*
25 FLO̶U̶R̶I̶S̶H̶I̶N̶G̶ ̶W̶O̶M̶E̶N̶

Joy
Recipes for
Abundance

"May you find some Joy' in each day', Love & hugs, Mom

INTRODUCED BY ★ SABINE MATHARU

This book has been written for information purposes only.
Every effort has been made to make this book as complete
and accurate as possible.

However, there may be mistakes in typography or content. Also, this
book provides information only up to the publishing date. Therefore, it
should be used as a guide – not as the ultimate source. The purpose of
this book is to educate.

The author and the publisher do not warrant that the information
contained in this book is fully complete and shall not be responsible for
any errors or omissions. The author and publisher shall have neither
liability nor responsibility to any person or entity with respect to any
loss or damage caused or alleged to be caused directly or indirectly
by this book.

*Thank you to my husband and
2 children Sasha and Sarina who continue to be
my true Joy and Inspiration in my life.*

*This book series has been "given to me as a mission"
to help empower women around the world.
Through this beautiful project, we are bringing joy
and happiness into our daily lives,
and touch thousands of other lives too as we
create a ripple effect around us.*

"Let's Reach For Greatness together."

- Sabine Matharu -

Joy

Jogging along the path I see
Outstretched arms and the skipping feet of
youngsters, so happy and screeching with glee.

Joyfully they play and how well I remember
Of times in my childhood, that tingling and energy
yes...a magical feeling into which I can surrender.

Just a thought can do it – bring it forth from within;
On the screen of my mind, I know what to do, for
yielding to that emotion of joy, it can again begin.

Journeying in life with those ups and downs,
Onward I struggled, at times without knowing that
yesterday's woes don't determine today's playground.

Jubilant I look on in pride at how far I have come,
Old stories no longer holding me to a time when I
yearned, for what I thought could never be done.

Joy, you were always there - a light of love and life within me;
Only my awareness, did I need to raise of so many delights
you bring each day for me to see.

Joy, joy, joy – what a feeling is this?
Oxygen to my being, a
youthfulness elixir of bliss.

❦ *by Susanne Wiechert* ❦

✿ REVIEWS ✿

I loved reading these stories about women sharing their journeys.
Once I started reading, I could not stop. This book is so motivating and
shows that anyone can turn their dreams into reality. I recommend this
book to anyone needing motivation or having roadblocks in their life.

- Michelle Paczesny -
Mum, Wellness Coach

This book made me pause and think about the quest for happiness
and if it was something I wanted in my life? Joy is something that
we rarely think about. Matthew McConahey, the famous actor talked
about the difference between joy and happiness in a speech he did
at Houston University.

He said that most of us just want to be happy, but being happy is usually
an emotional response to an outcome. It is something that we chase.
Whereas 'JOY' is something else - it is the feeling we have from doing
what we are fashioned to do. He admits, once he started to enjoy his
work, the accolades came and it stopped chasing the happiness train.
If I get this, I will be HAPPY - instead, he just enjoyed the journey.

The women in this book have truly harnessed what it is to live in JOY.
Their stories are phenomenally inspirational and will have you hooked
from the 'get go'.

I would suggest that anyone who is in the pursuit of happiness to take
a moment and listen to what JOY can do for you.

- Laura Ash -
Rock Solid, Wellness Coach

I thoroughly enjoyed reading the stories of women who have found joy in their daily lives. It strikes me, from reading their words, that joy is something that comes from within and is as unique and special as each of the women who have shared their tales so openly. A wonderfully inspiring read.

- Lucy Goodwill -

Portrait & Professional Branding Photographer

I am so grateful to each of the ladies who have shared their incredible stories. Each story is unique and touches a corner of life frequently buried and ignored. I particularly identify with Julie Sylvia Kalungi, having come from the same country moved abroad as adults. It is incredible what can be achieved once the blockers and limiting beliefs are removed.

- Brenda Jane Nakato -

Network Marketer & Property Proprietor

Utter brilliance! I was completely mesmerized and engulfed in the stories of these amazing and strong women. It was so uplifting reading through their story it made me realise how similar our difficulties. Reading their struggles and joys lifts me up and makes me want to push harder for my goals and dreams. I truly cannot wait to add "Joy – Recipes for Abundance" to my collection.

- Caroline Abela -

Diva Inside

❋ PREFACE ❋

I would like to say thank you to my family who have supported me throughout my entrepreneurial journey. My colleagues, friends, my mentors and all the amazing women that have come together to co-author this fabulous book and who share parts of their joy journey.

This series of books was born through inspiration and through taking inspired action. Loosing the fear of the unknown and stepping into my power. Following this incredible vision has not only brought me tremendous respect and visibility - but I have also been able to bring together the most amazing women on the planet who I dearly thank for so openly sharing their stories which I know will touch many more hearts and lives.

This to me is JOY! To know that with my contribution in this world, I am able to help others in their journey, to create something unique that brings people and communities together. I believe that when we act as a community, we have a much larger impact as opposed to when we act on our own. If we all do our 'bit' we will create shifts in people's consciousness that will create a more peaceful world.

As part of this wider vision, I help women in their businesses. I believe when women are fulfilled, they can live their lives around their family without stress and overwhelm, they can be better mums, better wives, better daughters. Their energy is contagious and it creates a ripple effect.

I have built my own business on the foundations of creating a fun passion business which doesn't create long hours and the feeling of being a 'slave' in your business. Instead, it centres around following a certain order and some foundational steps that will clear the path and make business activities so much easier and client attraction effortless.

To help deliver these results, I run several programmes and masterminds for different groups of entrepreneurs depending on what level they are in their business and what their preferred way of working is. One option is to join my signature programme, called 'The Business Accelerator Mastermind', where I develop and nurture ambitious women closely to achieve the success they deserve. A safe space which creates friendships and the opportunity to exchange ideas, get support and accountability as we implement.

Secondly, I also run "The Greatness Club", which helps women with growth, visibility and creating collaborative opportunities.

My 3 key values inside my programmes:

Growth

Consistently developing & implementing ideas and fine tuning ways to attract new clients. Another big aspect is automation, increasing impact and creating the income you deserve.

Visibility

Monthly online 'Speed Networking' events allow us to connect with potential clients where we are able to present what we do in business. The 'Reach For Greatness TV' and the 'Greatness Magazine' gives Club members a chance to become visible through being a contributor.

Community

Through Expert Q&As, I invite guest speakers into the Club on a monthly basis to provide quality training that can also lead to further collaboration with Club members.

You can get more information about the community and my programmes as well as special offers by singing up for the book bonuses on the next page.

Lastly, with everything I do at Reach For Greatness, it's about helping women create a balance in life and business, achieve their full potential and live their greatness as well as helping charitable organisations that are in need of funding. You will find the charities we support in the back of this book. In this way, we can do good together on a number of levels.

- Sabine Matharu -
Founder of Reach for Greatness

Joy

Recipes for Abundance

GRAB YOUR BOOK BONUSES TODAY

Fabulous bonuses have been selected for our gorgeous readers that will support you on the journey to Joy in your personal and business growth.

Please follow the link below.

REACH
FOR GREATNESS

✿ **www.learnmoreabout.info/joy** ✿

✿ CONTENTS ✿

SUNSHINE TROPICANA

1 Soft Luscious Beach

2 Tbsps of Sugar-Coated Sweethearts

5 Scoops Of Silliness

2 Squeezy Hugs

Unlimited Juicy Kisses

- Sabine Matharu -

CHILDHOOD MEMOIRS

During the 1980s, when Madonna was at top of the charts and Walkman, Commodore 64 and Joysticks were cool, I was around nine years old. It was early July and like every year, we were preparing for our family camping holiday. I was so excited to go on a road trip to the coast of Italy with my parents and my little brother. It was going to be an overnight car journey from Austria through the Swiss Alps toward Rimini to the Italian Riviera. By midnight the car and the trailer were fully loaded with camping gear and we were ready to hit the road.

One thing that I'll always remember from these road trips are the good old, cheesy tapes we used to play in the car. My mum usually dug them out a day or two beforehand – the songs of Dravi Deutscher, Albano & Romina Power and Neil Diamond were on my parent's favourite list. Whenever I stumble across these songs, I get butterflies in my stomach and the memories of these trips become alive again. I find it interesting how music can change your state of mind and trigger memories and feelings of certain times in your life.

I recall the bumpy journey as we climbed several mountains and stopped at the San Bernardino pass at over 2000m for a rest.

When we arrived the next morning, we were greeted by the old "Capo" – the boss who oversees the camp ground by paroling the grounds on his bike every hour. His strict Italian expression made him look very intimidating. Nobody wanted to get on the wrong side by disobeying the camp ground rules, especially my nine-year-old self!

Well, apart from a few times. On occasions when I had made some Italian friends and neither spoke each other's language, we would try to communicate in creative ways which ended up in lots of laughter. We would add silliness when we played games until late into the night, ride our bikes or hang out by the swings. Best of all were the arcade games. I fondly remember the flipper game machine, the marble maze and the motor race bike. I just couldn't get enough and continued to beg my parents for more coins.

On these camping trips, I learnt that one has to first build their tent as soon as they arrive before the fun can begin. It always puzzled me as there were so many pieces to assemble which seemed to take hours. I was impatient and eager to finally get to the luscious beach and feel the soft white sand between my toes. To me, beach, sun and sand are the best way to spend your day. Building sandcastles, eating ice creams and custard doughnuts followed by a game of Boccia. I call this pure joy!

Sometimes we would go sightseeing or visit the market where I'd get a new toy. In my adulthood, I still believe the greatest way to find joy is through travelling. This, for me, means getting to know new cultures, having new adventures and trying new food.

Just thinking back to these family camping trips makes me smile. I also recall hiking in the forest with my grandfather who would carve musical pipes for me out of wood or precious moments spent with my grandmother, my hero and inspiration who was such a free spirit. One day, the two of us felt very jolly as we sang our hearts out to karaoke standing on top of a plastic wash bowl!

Another joyful memory from my life is chilling on the beaches of Thailand where my boyfriend proposed in a romantic spot overlooking the beach followed by an intimate and beautiful wedding. Soon after, we were blessed to celebrate the birth of our son Sasha, followed by our daughter Sarina. I cannot express in words how much joy, new meaning and life purpose these children have brought into my life.

Of course, there is a challenging side to a young family, bills to pay, a career and running a business. Life was, and is, busy and at times can feel overwhelming. Yet I believe, we can find joy in an instant daily by simply conjuring up memories that make us feel happy and loved.

I find that there are always moments of joy and abundance available if you just allow yourself to slow down for a moment and put things into perspective. This certainly didn't come naturally to me but I have always been on the quest for a peaceful life with lots of happy moments rather than being stressed all day long. I had to learn to appreciate and celebrate all the wonderful things I had already achieved as opposed to continuously pushing for more and focusing on the lack of materialistic things I desired.

How many times have we told ourselves that our life will be better once we get that promotion, a more expensive car or a bigger house? How often do we race through life without taking a moment to stop and appreciate our sweethearts and friends around us serving up juicy kisses and hugs, instead of seeking entertainment and connection on social media?

I asked myself 'how do I experience joy and how can others experience joyful and carefree moments every day?' I notice that these moments seem to have been present and more appreciated when I was a child. Perhaps because there was less responsibility and less life pressure.

I believe joy happens when we are purely living in the moment. I think it is every child's intuition to seek great times by connecting with nature, being playful and creative as well as exploring new things.

When we go through life, remember who we are at heart, lose the fear of being judged and believe in our capabilities, we 'Reach For Greatness'. And when we finally silence self-doubt and fear of failure, we create a feeling of lightness and invincibility, subsequently unleashing and celebrating JOY and abundance.

SABINE MATHARU

BUSINESS START UP & GROWTH STRATEGIST

reachforgreatness.co.uk

Sabine Matharu is a passionate business start-up and growth strategist. She specialises in helping women find their purpose and monetise their unique skills so that they can build a thriving business with ease.

In addition she runs "The Empowerment Portal" for professional women, a platform hosting a wide range of experts who teach and coach on subjects including Mental and Physical Wellness, Leadership Tools and Career Coaching.

She is also the founder and host of the Women in Leadership Summit 2019 and 2020 as well as an international best-selling author of Rise - In Pursuit of Empowerment.

She firmly believes that it is possible to reach for the greatness within ourselves and expresses this through her programmes, wide range of charitable campaigns and collaboration projects.

CHRISTMAS CAREER CRACKERS

2 or 3 Sweet and Salty Crackers

1 Bag of Courage

2 Cups of Curiosity

2 Cups of Patience

2 Tbsps of Playfulness

1 Loving Mother or Close Friend

- Adriana Kosovska -

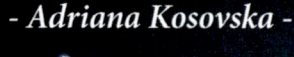

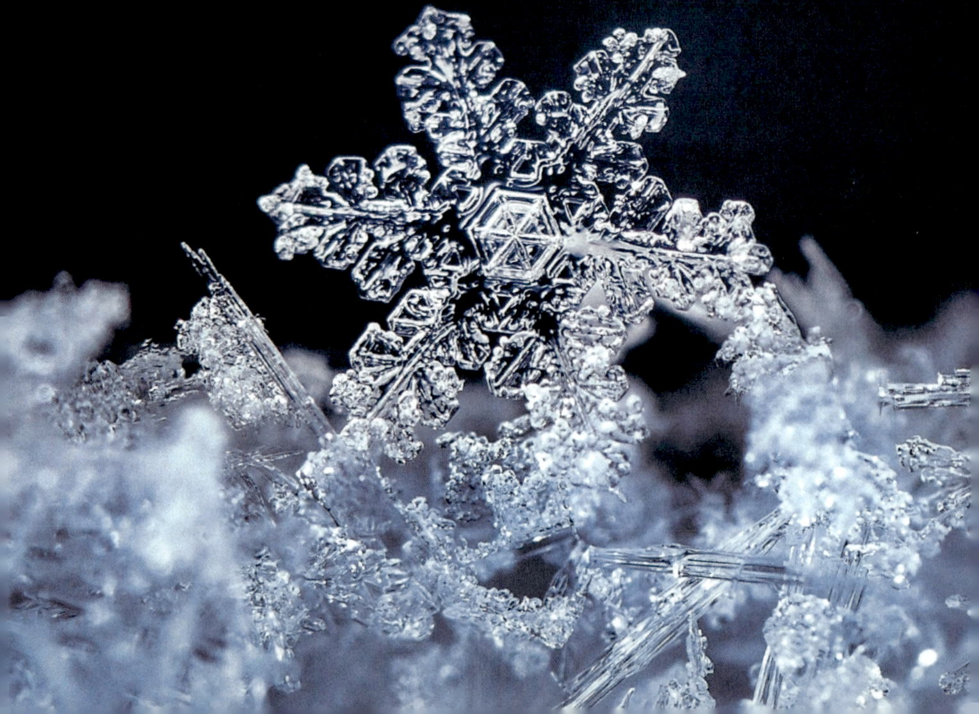

CHRISTMAS SURPRISE

It was Christmas 2013. I used to live in Southend on Sea in Essex and my mother had come to visit from Slovakia. Spending time with her was precious to me. Being together that Christmas was the best present I could ask for. Little did I know, my mum was about to give me the most life-changing gift.

"What's happening with you, my lovely? I no longer recognise the happy daughter I used to know" said my mum, just as we were preparing for the celebration. Her question confused me. It felt like taking a bite from a sweet and salty cracker, a taste I wasn't expecting. I thought that I had it all figured out. I moved to the UK with one suitcase and a heart full of dreams. I built great friendships and settled in well. I achieved my long-desired career dream. Life was good and I was happy...so I thought.

It seemed I didn't realise what was obvious to others. Long working hours and a blinkered commitment to excel in my career led me into the so-called 'rat race'. I began feeling tired and drained. I realised I was neglecting joy, creativity and passion, so I decided to make these powerful forces a priority in my life, especially in my working life.

Our conversation continued and I found the courage to say to my mother, "you know I would love to run my own business but I don't know where or how to start." She smiled and added, "you've been saying that for years and I've been waiting for the moment when you realise that you should finally start. I'm glad it's happening now."

A big smile appeared on my face. I was expecting all sorts of arguments against the idea such as 'are you crazy? Why would you want to give up your well paid job?' or 'Hmmm are you sure? It sounds too risky...' Instead my mum added, "if you don't try it, you'll never know. Plus, you have your finance career to fall back on!"

From that moment on, I felt empowered to explore what my business mission could be. I left my demanding managing role and got a part-time finance job. I started to organise sessions and workshops for women in our community and amazing things started to happen. We attracted more talented women to our community. I noticed that women often strived for well-paid jobs and looked up to well-known women from TV, magazines or social media who have different lives and life challenges. I wanted to help the women from our town connect with each other so they could find inspiration within their own life stories. Through a series of workshops, we found passion and inspiration, organised several conferences, raised money and supported charities. We had so much fun when we were together. I absolutely loved it.

Yet, I was still feeling empty in my finance career. Finance was all I knew. It started to bore me badly but I was paralysed by the fear of failure. I didn't know how to move forward or what else I could do.

My colleague asked me one day, "why don't you support employees in their careers? If it wasn't for you, I would have been stuck in the factory. You encouraged me to aim higher." I wasn't sure what she meant at first but she explained. "It can be difficult for an employee to grow and decide what to do next in their career. You are creative and have a passion for helping people. You're clearly an example that leading a successful career is possible".

I never thought of my own success in this way. I thought the opposite. I associated it with stress and burning out. She helped me to open my eyes and I started to connect the dots. I took it as a sign and launched my career coaching business on the side. I started to be playful and curious about how I could help employees to find joy and happiness in their careers. I started to write and blog, things I never thought I would be able to do.

I felt inspired, joyful and happy. My dating life transformed and I soon met my fiancé. My joy, fulfilment and passion for what I was doing started to shine through until others could see it too. New opportunities started to show up. Just when I thought about giving up my finance career, I got an offer to lead finance teams for a global corporation.

From the moment I made joy a top priority in my life, I not only experienced more of it but my life and career presented extraordinary and amazing opportunities. I went from being single and overworked to being fulfilled, recognised, valued and happily engaged.

Today I feel grateful that I recognised joy and made it a part of my life. It shows up in many different ways and what I value the most is that I learned to be more present with it, especially in my career.

I often hear that words like passion, excitement and inspiration don't belong to the world of business and employment. Yet, imagine how much better you would feel if your working days were filled with more joy, pleasure and fulfilment.

ADRIANA KOSOVSKA

FINANCE MANAGER, DREAM JOB COACH AND LEADERSHIP FACILITATOR

zerotodreamjob.com

Adriana Kosovska is a creative and enthusiastic change-maker. She has a passion for leadership, supporting people in finance careers and coaching employees to awaken their sleeping career potential.

Having seen too much frustration, disengagement and stress within the workplace, she made it her mission to help employees realize that they can build their dream careers instead of feeling like a number on a payslip. Adriana is not afraid to bring her human-oriented approach into global corporations.

Outside of work, she loves nature, coffee, spending time with her family and friends, hiking, arts, oil painting, exploring the world and of course celebrating Christmas.

SALTED CARAMEL SAUCE

9 Years of Motherhood

3 Beautiful and Amazing Children

A Large Bowl of Life Events

1 Helping of Grief

1 Helping of Joy

- Aishleen Cunningham

A SALTED CARAMEL LIFE

There is more than one way to make a cake. Like our unique tastes, we each have unique life experiences and these work to shape who we are and how we live our lives.

I am forty years old, a wife and a mum to three beautiful children. Our first daughter, now nine years old, was born healthy and well. Our second child was diagnosed twenty weeks into the pregnancy with a significant physical disability. She underwent several surgeries, multiple medical and physical challenges and has grown into a happy and confident six-year-old girl who is independent in her wheelchair. Our third child, my baby boy Rónan, died when he was just five months old. I was living every mother's worst nightmare and I thought I would never find joy again. I went through the deepest pains of grief, feeling it every step of the way.

Rónan's death slowly prompted an introspective journey into the depths of my soul. I read and learned so much about the way our thoughts shape our reality, how our mind is the gateway and our thoughts are the gatekeeper to the life we want to live.

One of the first books that made a real impact on me, during that first year of grief, discussed joy as being essential to a life well lived.

This made me stop and think. I didn't believe joy and grief could ever co-exist. They seemed too much in opposition. Two very different and contrasting experiences. It certainly didn't seem possible in the pits of grief that I would ever experience joy but thankfully in that dark place, there was a glimmer of light. It started as a tiny flicker and though I dismissed it plenty of times, I eventually opened my heart to the possibility of light and hope entering once again. Although joy and grief don't necessarily belong together, just like salt and caramel it was the taste of one that made the other more delicious. The joy I experience now is greater because of that contrast.

I still have my grief but I'm more attuned to feelings of love for my son and the blessings he continues to bring. With time and a lot of work (grief is hard work), I developed a deeper appreciation for life. Over nine years of lived experience and a vast amount of learning, I now know what works best for me and I feel passionate about helping others to do the same.

This led me to start up Mind-Body-You, a website of online resources and tools to support mums in creating their own recipes for joy and wellness. It has become my passion and purpose to create a nurturing space where I can help mums through the unique struggles of motherhood so they never have to feel lost or alone. Although shaped by my own mothering experiences, the resources can be adapted to be used by any mum, no matter where she is in her motherhood journey.

I certainly could have used these resources after my first child. Even though this experience of motherhood was my most 'typical', I still developed anxiety and found the adjustment to motherhood tough. I have always loved being a mum, and I have had so many joyful moments with each of my three children, getting lost in the depths of my love for them. Yet I remember feeling lonely, unsupported and struggling in the chaos of being a brand new mum. Like many, I had to adjust to unexpected changes in the way I was thinking (Mind), challenges to my physical recovery (Body) and how I felt within myself (You). The Mind-Body-You approach would have helped me greatly after all three of my children.

I believe that joy is found in the present moment, in being physically, mentally and emotionally in the 'here and now'. I spent so much time living in the past and the future that I struggled to be in the present moment. I now easily find my way to joy and my wish is that others feel equipped to do the same.

Joy can be found inside each of us and we can make it rise to the surface despite our unique circumstances. We just need to know where to look and how to find the right ingredients. Sometimes, it's about using and sourcing better tools or following a different method but everyone can taste joy again, even amidst grief or pain.

Joy for me now comes with immense love for my son. At my most joyful times, I feel I am connected with him and I feel appreciation for my whole family, my life and myself. I would describe joy as a sense of abundance, light and hope. It's like I've tapped into an eternal source of wellness.

Wellness is a powerful, and yet under-appreciated word, especially when it comes to motherhood. The meaning of 'wellness' and what that looks like in our day-to-day lives will be different for each of us. We all have unique lives, likes and experiences. Yet, despite these differences we are all so very connected. We share an understanding of what it is like to 'feel good' and can use this to guide us through each chapter of our lives.

Wellness helps us focus on joy and empowers us to take ownership of our well-being. It is ever evolving with the chapters of our life, and motherhood. Based on my own lived experience, I believe it is the key ingredient to a life of abundance and joy. It is so important that we know what wellness means to us and the simple ways we can achieve and maintain it.

AISHLEEN CUNNINGHAM

FOUNDER AND CREATOR OF MIND-BODY-YOU

mind-body-you.com

Aishleen is the founder and creator of Mind-Body-You.
With nine years of motherhood experience and many lessons
learned, she provides online tools and programmes, resources,
support and products for mums to bring balance, wellness and joy
into their lives.

Life's challenges have encouraged her to find the strength we all
have buried deep inside. Through various therapies, treatments
and educational study, she discovered a holistic system that would
bring wellness and joy into her own life.

Knowing she could have benefited herself from the
Mind-Body-You approach, her mission is to offer support
to all mums, regardless of their circumstances or particular
challenges so they too can enhance wellness, joy and balance
in their day-to-day lives.

SERENDIPITY SUNDAE

An Infinite Amount of Love,
Gratitude and Laughter

An Abundance of Self Belief,
Worthiness and Power

4 Beautifully Unique Children

6 Mischievous Grandchildren

Lashings of Approval, Acceptance and Forgiveness

A Strong Circle of Family and Friends

A Sprinkle of Magic, Miracles and Sparkle

- Angela Mercer -

RADIANT LIGHT

There was a time when looking back on my life filled me with a deep sense of failure. I had what many would see as an ideal family upbringing. I was the fourth of five siblings, born within six years. Life at home was lively, chaotic at times and filled with lots of laughter. Bright, mischievous and with a wicked sense of fun, I was not afraid to challenge the boundaries. I remember playing in the local woods, riding my bike and going on adventures. My father was big on adventures and every Sunday my parents would bundle us into the car, destination unknown and off we went.

I failed dismally at primary school. As the fourth child in succession moving through the same classes with the same teachers, I began to lose a sense of who I was. I would be called by my sister's names. Some days, they might even remember mine. Around the age of seven, our teacher asked us about the musical instruments we had at home. With excitement, my hand shot up. This was a question I could answer. I couldn't get it wrong. Straining frantically, the teacher exhausted all other hands until none remained but mine. Of course she had heard it all before. Her red-faced exasperation was evident even before I muttered the word 'violin'. "I have heard that three times now and I don't ever want to hear it again", she raged. I remember recoiling, shrinking within, feeling ashamed for speaking up, feeling ashamed by the sudden, brutal exposure to the class. I felt worthless and failure flashed like lightning through every part of me.

It was with sheer relief that I moved from primary to secondary school. I failed my entrance exam and started in the bottom sets. With tenacity and determination, within a year I moved into the top sets always focusing on achieving the next prize and finally the ultimate prize of Head Girl. Success seemed to flow into my life. However, beneath the surface lay a deep-seated fear that I wasn't enough, that I wasn't smart enough, that I didn't deserve to be seen or heard. Anxiety began to creep in like water seeping persistently and relentlessly through a leaking pipe.

I can remember with such intense joy the moment I was blessed with each of my four children. Seeing a young family grow is one of the greatest joys and also one of the greatest challenges. Working part-time and managing the ups and downs single-handedly during the week left me feeling depleted, empty and alone. As the children grew so did the problems until I had nothing left to give. No matter what I did, no matter how much energy, commitment and dedication I poured into my family, I was judged, blamed and criticised by professionals, teachers and friends for the growing dysfunction that had become family life.

I lost my marriage, my home and for several years, my two oldest children. I reeled in pain. I sank so low into that deep, dark abyss called depression that living each day seemed inconceivable. I felt numb. I felt worthless. I felt powerless. My children needed me, yet I felt I had failed everyone. For two long years I fought, I resisted, I struggled. I blamed the absence of the man I loved for taking away my power and self worth. How dare he leave without warning, without discussion, without an explanation?

Yet the simple truth was, no-one had taken my power from me. He had been a good father and a good husband. Like me, he just couldn't cope. Slowly, something shifted within. I had been so busy being a wife and a mother, so busy putting everyone's needs before my own that I had forgotten who I was. Self-love and self-care weren't notions I had contemplated. In fact, quite the opposite. I had always held the mistaken belief that putting my own needs first was selfish. With this new awareness came acceptance and with acceptance came the power of knowing that I had achieved peace within myself, peace with the situation and peace in that moment.

Suddenly, an inner light began to flicker and glow. As I forgave myself and learnt to love and accept myself unconditionally, that beam of light has grown ever stronger allowing me to reclaim my power, my worth and my joy.

In the last thirteen years, I have had life experiences beyond what I thought possible. Just as the loss of my marriage, our home and children was like a tsunami knocking me into hidden, turbulent waters, I have been washed away over and over again, each time emerging stronger and more resilient than ever before. I no longer try to figure out the 'whys'. They are not important to me as each challenge has brought me to a new understanding of who I am and why I am here.

Joy comes from finding the peace within ourselves, to be ourselves, to love ourselves and to honour ourselves. When we understand this great truth then our light can radiantly shine through. Now, I look back at my life with compassion, kindness and forgiveness – for myself and others. After all, we all do the best we can with what we know in any given moment. To judge anyone for past mistakes would also be to judge myself.

I have the deepest gratitude for my four beautiful children, six mischievous grandchildren, a circle of cherished family and friends and those I have loved and lost for bringing me to where I am today. You are my greatest teachers, my inspiration and my joy. We are the magic and the miracle.

I feel blessed to have walked in the darkness because out of that darkness I learnt to find the light and to cultivate a lasting joy that comes from within. My purpose and passion is to share this gift with others, to help them rediscover who they are, to value their worth, to reclaim their power and to live a life of freedom and joy.

ANGELA MERCER

TRANSFORMATIONAL COACH, CLINICAL HYPNOTHERAPIST, TEACHER AND TRAINER

angelamercer.co.uk

Angela inspires clients to reach beyond their limitations, to own their worth, to truly love and accept themselves unconditionally and to become the truest, most authentic version of themselves. This leads to greater success in relationships, careers, finances and health.

She passionately believes when turning life experiences into gifts something profound happens for us. Angela combines over 25 years of teaching and training with coaching, life visioning and hypnotherapy to produce powerful, transformative results.

Through her own experiences, Angela has learnt to go beyond happiness to a place where she is so connected and peaceful within, allowing her to live her purpose and achieve her highest potential - this can be you too. Angela has found her inner light, her anchor; that beautiful three-letter word 'joy' - which means 'darkness expelled'. It is now her passion and her mission to inspire you to find your own 'joy', to reclaim your power and to live of your dreams.

JOY TRAIL MIX

1 Handful of Blue Sky

*1 Scoop of Wild Coastline, Open Meadow
and Deep Dark Woods*

A Dash of Forgiveness

1 Pair of Boots

Trail Guide or Map (Optional)

- Anastacia Keogh -

REWILDING THE JOYFUL SOUL

When my two children were five and three, I found myself a single mum. It's something I feared would happen and it did. What would I do for money? How could I look after them and work? How would I get my oldest son who is autistic the help he needed? I am a trained actor and came to the UK to realise the dream of being an international actor and storyteller. But my margin for success was so narrow, and I too often compared myself to others who I deemed successful. With the advent of social media, it seemed I could never be good enough. Not as an artist, not as a mother and this was my second failed marriage. A brilliantly talented fuck-up. I didn't even have a proper job. I had stints as a 'resting' actor when I worked as an education officer at Kew Gardens (a role my mother, a wildlife volunteer, painter and photographer was endlessly proud of) and in advertising agencies. But how could I do those jobs in London and make the school run?

I didn't have time to feel sorry for myself. I was too busy monetizing my talent into something that would bring home the bacon so I could fry it in a pan. I did a teacher inset for a posh boarding school and they asked me to set up a LAMDA (London Academy of Music and Dramatic Arts) program to teach and coordinate acting, voice and speech examinations. Thus began a 15-year career as a shadow artist and running around in a hamster ball growing a business as a LAMDA teacher with five different schools. I taught over 350 students and sometimes worked seven days a week. Feast and Famine. Time for Money. I have such gratitude for the childcare people who helped me bridge the gaps. They were usually sixth-formers who were utterly wonderful at helping the kids with homework, sorting out squabbles and managing the house.

One day, I came home to the kids from working an incredibly busy day seeing student upon student. The babysitter noticed. 'You don't look so well, do you want me to stay'? - 'No it's ok...come on, I'll give you a lift home. I just have a splitting headache.' When I returned home, I took my bags upstairs and collapsed in a heap on the floor. I couldn't get up and I couldn't stop sobbing. I had no idea what was going on and I scared my daughter so much that she went and got a neighbour who told me to go and see the GP. Exhaustion. Stress. I got some support (another appointment to keep) and tablets so I could carry on with my mad schedule. Being self-employed in this gig economy means if you don't work, you don't get paid and you lose your contract.

When the kids went to their dad's for the week, I appealed to a friend who had a special place she went to every year to meet friends in Cornwall. It's a little fishing village right on the South Coastal Trail. Heaven! I had to work through a lot of fear. Making arrangements for accommodation last minute, driving the six hours to get there and allowing myself the luxury of spending money on myself. I felt I had to have a plan so I created a walking agenda with various destinations each day, building up to the penultimate 20-mile hike around the Lizard Peninsula. Just me, my boots, the sea and the trail. It took me back to the amazing hikes and mountaineering adventures with my university buddies in Boulder, Colorado. I re-tasted the pleasure of hiking with my Mum, exploring the Olympic Peninsula and hiking with a tide chart in La Push, Washington. I felt myself coming back to my soul. My shoulders dropped, the scales over my eyes fell away. I began to experience a sort of...joy. I stopped having an agenda. The next year, I made it up as I went along. I took side trips to explore places I read about in books like Jamaica Inn, Tintagel Castle and Frenchman's Creek. I met people there who became friends for life. I came back year after year to walk and talk. The atmosphere was warm, accepting and friendly. It reminded me of the lake in Michigan where my grandparents built a cottage in the 50s. It was a childhood idyllic place of family, freedom and fun that we now share with our children. It is my happy place, the one I visualise in meditations.

Teaching every hour that God sent became unsustainable. I began to focus on a new business of storytelling in the corporate world. However, businesses take a while to develop and grow. My finances took a dive and my daughter, who was always my little star, became my teenage nightmare challenging me on every level. She taught me a lot about killing off the 'good girl' and letting go. Yet it was tough and hurtful. I felt like a bad mother who had neglected her needs while focusing on the special needs of my son. I didn't make it to Cornwall for two years or home to the lake of my childhood memories and my loving, supportive family although they sent money to tide me over. I retreated into a deep hole of shame. Not successful but a brilliantly talented fuck-up once again. I didn't deserve a holiday. I couldn't show my face and admit what a failure I was.

Like the ugly duckling in the story, a hard winter or three ensued. In the interim I started wild swimming. It was a call from the wild directly to my soul. I was working on Selkie (seal people) stories at the time so I took a deep breath and dove in. Physically going through the motions of going with the flow and allowing myself to be held by water restored peace, confidence and joy within me.

My daughter has now moved in with her dad and is doing well in a college program, scooting around on a Vespa and working like the independent young woman she's always wanted to be. My son is accepting his role into adulthood slowly. I returned to the lake under bitter-sweet circumstances as my father passed away to join my mother who left us on Christmas Eve, 10 years ago. I'm considering buying a lake property, my little piece of joy and a place I can always go home to. After a two-year absence from Cornwall, I picked up the phone and booked a room in my favourite B&B. I chose 'The Juliet' room with a balcony overlooking the cove that I swim in each day, reuniting with my Cornish family. I realise now the joy these things bring into my life inspires not just me but everyone I interact with. I have brought joy into my business; infusing it into my clients and colleagues. I found out that abundance and joy reside at the same frequency. Finances are starting to flow. Oh, and I was awarded one of the annual Purple Shoe Awards from my business club Sister Snog for Most Joyful Sister this year. Go figure!

ANASTACIA KEOGH

STORYTELLER AND FOUNDER OF STORY PREZ

storyprez.co.uk

Anastacia Keogh is a storyteller with a diverse and rich background performing traditional tales with a contemporary twist, voice-over acting, coaching and training. Everyone has a story to share. Stacia enables people to discover, design and deliver their story. She mentors business owners and leaders in how to use the power of voice and language in a story structure to create a lasting impression and inspire listeners to take action. She coaches, speaks and runs workshops and webinars.

Stacia offers 1:1 coaching, pitch coaching for incubator and accelerator cohorts and presentation masterclasses online and in London. She works with clients to address fears and reinforce natural ability to illuminate messages through clear, concise purpose-told stories. She attracts like-minded people to come together as members of a tribe – be they clients, collaborators or communities.

In re-writing her own story of Lone Wolf and the Starving Artist she calls to others to shift their paradigm and share their gifts with us all.

JOY PAVLOVA

1 Handful of Photos
(Displaying Happy Moments and People You Love)

1 Gratitude Journal

1 Pen or Pencil

1 Music Device
(that can be turned on anywhere)

- Asya Barskaya-Lebed -

FINDING BLISS IN TIMES OF DARKNESS

Once upon a time, I was a very sad person and there was virtually no joy in my life. If you had a snapshot of me 12 years ago, you'd see me lying in bed with no energy, crying and feeling sorry for myself. I felt like my life had no meaning and I was dying. The only thing keeping me going was my son. He was only two years old at the time and I knew he needed me.

I loved him more than anyone or anything in this world and I wanted to be able to look after him. To do that I had to first take care of myself. I made a decision that no matter what, I'd find happiness again and give my son the most wonderful life he could ever have. I came across Paul McKenna's Change Your Life In Seven Days CDs and started listening to them, focusing on moments of joy and happiness in my life.

Luckily, I have very few lasting memories of those sad years but one thing I remember enjoying amidst the pain was taking photographs of my little boy. I recall chasing him around the house, on the streets and in the park to snap a photo. I wanted to catch him and those moments with my camera so I could remember his cute little face forever. However, my camera was very basic and slow and it was rather frustrating.

I took the plunge and booked myself in for a weekend photography course. I suddenly felt alive and excited, like I was waking up from a very long and deep nightmare. Straight after the course, I ordered the best camera I could afford. I spent all my spare time practising and taking photos of family members, my friends and their children, my neighbours and even strangers!

I will never forget the overwhelming happiness that filled my heart when my shots started improving. I remember trying to work in the office and all I could think about were photographs I had already taken and photographs I wanted to take. I remember all the positive reactions from my friends whose children I practiced on. Even now they tell me that the photos I took back then are some of their favourite photos of their children.

13 years later, after going through numerous life challenges including divorce, redundancy, health issues, single parenthood and the instability of self-employment, my life has gradually transformed. Every day is filled with joyful moments. I am there for my son when he needs me and he sees a happy person who is always full of energy and life. We've been travelling in many countries and have shared many marvellous moments together. I am so proud of the way my son is growing up.

I am constantly surrounded by positive people and my photography is going from strength to strength. Sometimes, I want to pinch myself when I think of how I have my own business and I no longer need to work for somebody else. It's an incredible blessing to be paid for doing what you love. I meet many inspirational people and I sincerely love all my clients for giving me a chance to photograph them. My portraits help my clients see how beautiful they are and that also brings me a lot of joy.

I especially love working with children. I have a gift for connecting with them and making even the most quiet and shy children smile. Those smiles melt my heart and every time I look at a successful image, I feel the joy sparkling around me. It's also an immense joy to see my work published in magazines, displayed on walls in people's homes, printed on banners and shared on social media. Some days, there are thousands of people looking at my photographs and it feels so good. I deeply believe that joy is contagious and that my photographs, which are charged with love and positive energy, are helping to spread joy and make this world a happier place.

While photography occupies the largest part of my life, there are plenty of other joyful things that I get to experience. I love salsa dancing, travelling (especially to see my family in Russia), cooking for friends, baking with my son, walking, sunsets, learning languages, watching films, giving compliments, listening to music and laughing. I keep a gratitude journal which helps me focus on the blessings and attract more joy and abundance into my life.

When I look back on my time of darkness, I was clearly being pointed to the light. I listened to my heart and went on doing the one thing I enjoyed, even while deeply unhappy. It's important to be aware of your feelings and focus on things that evoke joy. When something feels good, take note of it. The more you focus on the things that bring you joy, the more joy will appear in your life.

ASYA BARSKAYA-LEBED

PROFESSIONAL PHOTOGRAPHER

ablphotography.co.uk

Asya Barskaya-Lebed is a portrait and commercial photographer based in Berkshire. She loves to spread joy through her photographs, which are charged with the spirit of happiness and positivity.

Born in Russia in the 70's with a very modest upbringing behind the Iron Curtain, Asya managed to leave the Soviet Union through some very lucky and unusual events. Taking the opportunity to study and travel in different countries including China, France and the USA, she finally settled in the UK and set up ABL Photography in 2007.

Asya is the mother of a 15-year-old boy who was her reason for striving to find joy and fulfilment in her life. She has designed her business in a way that allows her to be there for her son and follow her passion at the same time.

ABL Photography has helped several local and nationwide charities with fundraising, and she is working on other projects to help various charities raise funds and achieve their objectives.

A JOYFUL RIDE

1 Voice

1 Favourite Song

4 Cups of Willingness

1 Cup of Good Intentions

1 Heap of Love

1 Heap of Passion

5 Vowel Sounds to Warm Up Your Voice and Surrender

1-2 Creative Practices Daily

- Aurélie Lemière -

SOUL SONG

Singing and playing music with people bring tremendous joy into my life. When I found my true authentic voice and remembered that it was one of my favourite gifts to share with the world, I knew I had found joy for life. I had a big breakthrough one day during a sound journey at a festival and I couldn't stop crying as I realised how much time I wasted with my negative limited beliefs. I had been conditioned to believe I wasn't good enough, a belief which prevented me from sharing the gift I had since I was a little girl. This realisation was a deeply emotional and heartfelt moment. I remembered so clearly how I used to sing on a microphone and dance in my bedroom all the time as a child.

I was living in Cape Town when I first experienced joy as a grown-up. I wrote my first song called Peaceful Change, a healing song for the world to sing about inner peace and world peace. I sang it to everyone I encountered on my path. I'd share it at the market, gas stations, public places, beaches, open streets, events and festivals. I performed the song with several gospel choirs which uplifted me with such empowering joy. When I launched Voice The Change Global Peace Movement and a crowd-funding campaign 'A Call for Joy', I also launched the song to the world. It was the 12th February 2016, Valentine's Day weekend, so the song was especially perfect as it's about love, forgiveness and moving forward together. Its purpose enabled me to facilitate leadership workshops in underprivileged communities.

Since then, it has been my personal healing song and I truly believe we all have one in our hearts that we are born with. If we are just willing to listen and allow it to flow through us, we will hear it. You can sincerely feel joy in your whole being when finding your true voice and your own soul song.

Every time I sing, play music and perform, it is a joyful heart-warming moment. Every time I share songs of light, songs of the heart and run soul-singing and creative musical expression workshops, everyone in the group experiences joyful and magical moments to be remembered. I also see and receive confirmation that life is truly a miracle!

Being a peace activist and organizing peace events in Cape Town such as International Day of Peace, Global Oneness Day and One Billion Women Rising taught me a lot about how important it is to feel peace, joy and love within ourselves to experience it in the world around us. During these special events and sacred ceremonies in South Africa or during personal meditative moments, I received insights into the reality that we are all one. We are a connected, interrelated, interdependent human family. You are a part of it. We are all part of this giant web of life. It often saddens me to witness the spirit of separation, competition, hate, discrimination and absence of humanity in our society.

Some of my most emotional moments have been over losing loved ones who have been part of my journey. Change-makers like Nelson Mandela, John Oliver, Johnny Clegg, Michael Jackson, Bob Marley, John Lennon, M.L King, Robin Williams and Prince. I know their spirits are still alive as I feel their presence from high above. Being aware of this has made me wiser, stronger and more knowledgeable. As I experience grief, death and rebirth, I feel myself expand and evolve. My work with Voice the Change has made me understand that the inner-work I do as an individual also has a global impact. I've seen it concretely happen in my life.

I firmly believe that if we allow ourselves to be authentic and positive in all situations without fearing judgement, if we embrace our uniqueness and allow our happy mood to prevail no matter what, we are empowered to be more confident and more loving towards ourselves. We step out of society's box and learn to value ourselves and be who we truly are: a beautiful valuable diamond filled with joy, love, peace, harmony and abundance.

What does this happy attitude do? What positive impact does it have? It inspires others to do the same. We need more joy catalysts in our world. Climb on board and join me. Join us to be catalysts of positive change and let's lead the world forward to make it a better place for all.

Singing to my mother, to my sisters and brothers and beautiful Mother Nature is a true divine healer to me and to them. When I sing or lovingly talk to the flowers, fruits and vegetables in the garden or to the trees, they thank me by growing, blossoming and being ready to be harvested. Receiving this ripple effect in delicious abundance of love and joy from nature is true love in action. Let's plant these seeds of joy, love and peace everywhere to voice the change because it is possible. 'Let's move forward together'.

What is your soul song?

AURÉLIE LEMIÈRE

JOY CATALYST & EMPOWERMENT COACH, FOUNDER OF VOICE THE CHANGE

voicethechange.co

Aurélie Lemière, founder of "Voice The Change" Global Peace Movement, is a Joy Catalyst & Empowerment Coach. She is also a singer/songwriter and a musician/accordionist and has released a new version of her song "Peaceful Change".

She is passionate about helping you to find your true authentic powerful voice while overcoming your fear of public speaking in order to gain self-confidence, self-worth and self-assurance. She does this using her favourite tools such as singing, playing music, soul sound healing, dancing, creative expression of voice and body and authentic relating.

Aurélie enjoys making a positive impact during her transformative workshops and retreats by assisting people who are going through life transitions or experiencing emotional distress or burnout. Her events are always interactive, vibrant, illuminating, and refreshing.

Her selfless work to inspire, uplift and empower communities demonstrates her most important life values: Love & Compassion.

JOYFUL LIVING

Jugs of Colour

One Loving Heart

Your Authentic Self

Fun Times with Family & Friends

Unlimited Gratitude

Lots of Adventures

- Caroline Emile -

AN ADVENTURE IN BAKING

It's been just over two weeks since I was laid off from my 'dream job'.

Before you get upset for me, let me clarify that I was actually relieved when my boss told me the news that Thursday! Sure, I was shaken by the uncertainty that now lay ahead of me but at the same time, I felt in my core that God was redirecting me to something better. I'd been quite unhappy at work in the last two to three months leading up to this moment.

In fact, it had reached the point where I would dread Sunday mornings (the first day of the working week in Egypt). I'd stay awake until the early hours, desperately trying to hold on to the remainder of my weekend before returning to the job and company that I'd grown to loathe. I told myself that I wasn't a quitter and that I would at least make it to my first year anniversary before resigning, overriding the negative impact this was having on my soul. So when I was abruptly released from my self-imposed 'incarceration' four months earlier than planned, my soul intuitively rejoiced! I positively embraced the blank canvas that lay ahead of me, pushing aside looking for a new job to instead nurture my bruised soul.

So today I've decided to bake some cupcakes, simply because I can! I finally have ample free time to reconnect with my creativity, which had pretty much been shelved for over a decade with the limited 'spare time' available in my 9 to 5 corporate career lifestyle. Today I'm yearning to relive the joys of baking that I used to experience as a pre-teen in Home Economics class at school.

Off I head to the supermarket to get my ingredients for gluten-free cupcakes. I soon discover the complexities of trying to source supplies for a British recipe in an Egyptian supermarket. Gluten-free ingredients aren't as readily available here as they are in the UK. There's also a language barrier for me as I'm not fluent in 'cooking Arabic'. Not to worry, I can consult Google Translate. Oh, nothing's coming up for caster sugar. That's fine. I soon read the dictionary definition and try to match this with what's displayed on the shelves. I'm unable to find a close match and opt for a pack labelled 'powdered sugar' in Arabic, which I take to mean icing sugar (the closest fit I find for caster). See, that wasn't too bad. Wait...now I'm not sure if cornmeal flour is entirely gluten-free (allergens are not listed in Egypt). It's ok, I'll take the risk and assume that it's just pure cornflour without any additives.

Having overcome these preparatory hurdles, I'm now rearing to get on with my cupcake challenge! To my great astonishment, I soon discovered that my grandmother – in whose kitchen I'm staging my experiment, given her status as an avid baker – doesn't own any cupcake trays. I'm astounded!

Not wanting to abandon my core objective of baking, I quickly go online and look for alternative recipes not requiring cupcake trays. I opt for a simple sponge cake and a flourless walnut sponge cake. Stumbling across the latter is a good opportunity to not have to use the cornmeal flour that I was uncertain about. Now I'm finally off! I mix sugar with butter and flour, separate egg yolks from whites, chop and process walnuts and zest a lemon. I find peeling the lemon the hardest. Oh, and the fact that my grandmother doesn't own any measuring or weighing tools! Instead I had to plod my way through using empty water bottles and an array of different sized glasses and mugs.

I first bake the sponge cake. When I joyfully remove it from the oven less than 90 minutes after kick-off, my thirst for creation is still unquenched and so I proceed to also make the flourless walnut sponge. An hour or so later, I'm looking at my two creations while they sit cooling on the kitchen table. I feel a great sense of pride and joy with my accomplishments. I reflect on the experience I just had and extract the below lessons.

I can achieve anything I set my mind to. Despite the numerous obstacles I encountered, I didn't get easily deterred from my objective of baking which was something my soul called out for me to do.

Through flexibility, there's always an alternative path to joy. Although I originally set out to bake cupcakes, when faced with challenges I simply adapted the details of my plan rather than abandoned the idea of baking altogether.

There are opportunities in the midst of setbacks. Whilst I failed to make cupcakes today, I learnt how to make various types of sponge cakes and how to zest a lemon. I can still attempt making cupcakes on a future occasion but in my pursuit of this goal, I've enriched my skills.

I may not know exactly what I'm doing at all time but unchartered territory can definitely be exciting! I wasn't able to measure or weigh my ingredients and so wasn't able to accurately follow my chosen recipes. Yet plodding on as best as I could with the various sized mugs and glasses and using 'guesstimates' was actually fun. I enjoyed the sense of challenge and adventure I had on the way. As long as the general objective is clear, the small details don't have to be perfectly accurate as I can trust my instincts to fill in the gaps.

I'm the only judge needed of my achievements. Undoubtedly, the cakes didn't come out perfectly given the challenges I faced but I was absolutely delighted with them! Only I knew what I'd gone through to achieve the end results and I was certainly proud of what I'd accomplished. I'd wanted to bake for my own pleasure and not to impress others, therefore the experience I had mattered far more to me than the final outcome.

So next time you bake, mow the lawn, iron or whatever other 'ordinary' activity you pursue, switch off autopilot and connect with all your senses. Truly engage in the simple joys available within each moment without being attached to the outcomes. Ultimately, happiness doesn't need much to materialise. Simply choose to experience it in whatever you do, regardless of any challenges!

CAROLINE EMILE

HAPPINESS AND FULFILMENT COACH, SPEAKER AND AUTHOR

butterflyme.co.uk

Egyptian-born Caroline is a global citizen who currently lives in London. She is co-author of Voices Of Hope and winner of the Powerhouse Global Award - Inspirational Woman Of The Year 2019.

Caroline is on a mission to inspire and empower individuals on every continent to unleash the best - or butterfly - version of themselves, creating a happier and a more conscious world.

She professionally trained as a coach at the Co-Active Training Institute in London after working for almost a decade in marketing communications across various industries in the UK and Middle East.

A breast cancer diagnosis a few years later prompted Caroline to pursue her passion more zealously. Having experienced first-hand the detrimental effects of an unbalanced 9-5 lifestyle, she overcame her introverted nature to become a speaker, ensuring that her message to live purposefully reached more corporate careerists across the world.

INFINITE POSSIBILITY

❀

Oodles of Grit

Healthy Helping of Resilience

Cups of Compassion

Dollop of Strength

❀

- Cathy McKinnon -

THE MAGIC WITHIN

Do you remember that lightless feeling as a child, the sun beaming down on your face as you played outside, not a care in the world? The laughter and smiles consuming your days, pure joy.

As we get older and are exposed to life events, responsibilities and demands on our time, the weight on our spirit gets heavier, we laugh less often and smiles are at times forced. As our stress levels increase, our focus can wander from our goals and we become complacent in our daily schedules.

What causes this shift, how do we get back to that feeling of joy?

As children, we are taught the simple concept of following directions. It seemed following the path your family or mentors advised would inevitably lead to success which in theory would bring the return of that joy we felt as a child. I thought if I listened to them, if I followed their guidance and if I played safe I would be happy. I was taught to go to college, get a degree and get a good job. It's how success was measured and it was the path one was to take!

While those around me doubted my path and some told me I would not be successful, I dove headfirst into my career to prove them wrong. I worked multiple jobs, purchased a home and pushed through long days because I thought that was what I was supposed to do, that this was what success looked like.

But why did I still feel empty and alone? I thought this is what was meant to be fulfilling me and since I was supposed to see this as success, I hid my struggles from everyone. At one point I was hiding my depression by doing what I did best, grinding and hustling to hide the pain. My family praised success so I thought I'd give them success and hide the fact that I really thought I was a failure.

After my angel baby was born, what should have been the happiest time of my life turned into a living nightmare. A game of survival began in my household with explosive arguments, verbal abuse and a constant not knowing what I would come home to. When I finally started to open up to those around me about the hell I was living in, they were shocked. It appeared from the outside we had it all. My partner and I both had good careers, we had a nice house, a pool and a new baby. All we seemed to be missing was the white picket fence. However, inside those four walls, a very different story played out, it was extreme volatility. The stress was taking its toll on my health and my ability to manage all that was on my plate.

When you are living in fear and anxiety you not only lose sight of your true self but it also seems like that joyful feeling is beyond reach. I felt like I was drowning and fighting like hell to keep bobbing my head above water, gasping for air. I kept hoping for the moment when I could breathe again.

I couldn't allow my son to be raised in such a toxic and negative environment. It took me five years of trying for a baby to hold my son in my arms, so I would do what I had to do - to protect him. He deserved better, so I made some extremely challenging decisions and leaned into them. It was time to get my son out of this environment and that meant starting from a clean slate.

As a child you never truly understand the world around you or why you are in certain situations. Now I know that while I was frustrated with hanging out with my brothers and not being the princess, it gave me the grit, perseverance and strength for the situations I was about to handle. It was preparing me for what was ahead. While they wanted nothing but the best for me, the family members that doubted me were triggered into fear by my vision because it was an unknown path. Indeed, it was an unknown path.

However, it was not the END.

My world wasn't ending, in fact it was just beginning! I overhauled everything in my life: a new house, a new state, a new tribe of friends, new habits and a new mindset. It was a fresh start for my son and I. I found ways to incorporate this new way of living into our busy schedules. I became clear headed, less stressed and smiled more than I had in years.

It took many years of trial and error, frustration, depression and impatience but my son and I had arrived into our new way of life. It wasn't perfect but the number of days that included laughter were more than ever. I started to reconnect with my friends and do more things for myself, something I hadn't done in ages due to the chaos that had become my life. I discovered yoga, I laughed more than I cried, I enjoyed bike rides with my son, we went on adventures without the heaviness I previously carried. It took standing my ground on some very challenging decisions but I knew my path was bigger. I knew the only way was forward.

It wasn't always pretty. The sleepless nights, the tears and the frustration all lead me to where I am now. It was a definite awakening to what was truly important in my life, what I wanted out of life and what I wanted to teach my son. I wanted to show him that when we follow our true calling, joy will shine through in ways you never thought possible.

It was this series of events that shook me to the core and made me realize how I wanted to live and build my legacy. The lessons I learned were invaluable and something you cannot learn in a classroom. The strongest, bravest woman I've ever known said to me, "you hold down the fort and you do what you have to do for your family but remember to laugh along the way because life can get awfully serious".

Today, my spirit is continuously lifted by the shift I see in my clients. I use my lessons learned, my mess and my struggles to share with others that it is possible to find joy through the darkness. The knowledge I have gained through experience and education allows me to help women navigate how to find their magic again.

When you are in alignment with your calling, the joy will shine through you to those around you.

CATHY MCKINNON

TRANSFORMATION STRATEGIST

wellnesswarriorcoaching.com

As the founder of Wellness Warrior Coaching, Cathy McKinnon works with strong, courageous, motivated and ambitious women who are tired of drudging through the motions and are ready to take their lives to the next level. She shares her learnings through infertility, cancer and divorce to help other women avoid the same pitfalls she did and start to show up as their authentic selves.

Her combination coaching works to transform habits, routines, accountability and mindset to find joy, confidence and energy to propel them towards the optimal vision for their life.

Cathy is a co-author in Silent Grief, Healing & Hope, sharing her infertility journey along with 14 other women. The book, which reached Amazon's #1 bestsellers list, shares stories of healing after infertility issues, miscarriage and child loss that will captivate your heart, inspire you and offer hope.

JOY MESS WITH A CHERRY ON TOP

❋

500g of Spontaneity

1 Cube of Not Taking Yourself Too Seriously

1 Pinch of Glitter

1kg of Pure, Organic Self Love

One Shiny and Ripe Red Cherry

❋

- Debora Luzi -

A VERY FREEZING MOMENT

I never imagined, not in my wildest dreams that I, Debora the Queen of Drama would one day happily write about my journey with joy. Joy never existed in my dictionary. I always believed it was a very rare ingredient, so exotic and expensive that I could never get hold of it unless I travelled the world or was reborn into a new life. My mum always taught me that happiness and joy were only for rich and lucky people. We were not lucky or rich so I assumed this ingredient must be very expensive and impossible to access for a small town girl like me.

Like every child, I started to crave the very thing that I couldn't have. Joy became like a forbidden fruit. I started to write a diary at the age of eight as a way of coping with my reality, which definitely lacked joy and was fuelled by a lot of drama. Drama on the contrary was a very cheap ingredient for me. Highly accessible, available and of which I often overindulged. Looking back on those years, I never realised that I had tasted joy but I did not recognise it as such.

Some years later, I was living in a lovely two-bedroom flat with my two-year-old son. I had bought a flat in London as a single mother after being told by the council that I had to wait at least 15 years to be given a council house.

"Sorry madam, there's nothing I can do. Your points are very low."

I remember putting the phone down and crying like a baby. My little one came to me and gave me one of the biggest hugs he had ever given me and asked me why I was crying. As I dried my tears and looked straight into his eyes I said, "these are tears of joy because Mama has now decided that we will buy our own house".

Two years from that day I kept my promise and bought a two bedroom flat in central London. I remember saying yes to the estate agent and handing him a £250 cheque as a deposit. I felt so much joy and because I wasn't used to it, I had a terrible headache that night. The joy stayed with me for a while.

I was once asked to go back in time and remember the first time I felt a deep joy in my life. I was surprised when my mind took me back to a beautiful freezing day in April in that flat with my son. It was a cold Sunday morning when the doorbell rang. I answered the bell and realised that the delivery I was waiting for was finally here. I screamed from the excitement and my son, not knowing exactly what was going on, started screaming with me.

I opened the door and we ran downstairs with him behind me making all these joyful screams and funny noises like an excited animal in a jungle. There, in front of me was our beautiful garden table and chairs. I don't think the delivery man had ever seen such happy faces before. I went back into the house and I assembled the furniture quickly. I put them on the balcony and started making breakfast.

I had always wanted a balcony. I'd lived in many different flats in London over the past 20 years and none of them had one. I remember visiting the house of a friend and asking her if we could sit on the balcony even though it was freezing.

The cold on that day, the goosebumps on my skin, the teeth slightly shaking didn't bother me at all while I sat outside and ate breakfast with my son on our very own balcony. My son smiled at me and shivered. I asked him if he wanted to go inside and he said "No Mami. I am so happy here." I felt exactly the same. The joy was so intense that we forget about how cold it was and we enjoyed every single freezing moment of it.

The balcony that day felt like a 100m2 garden. The true secret of happiness is to saviour the joy that the smallest things in life can give you. I can still taste that feeling of utter joy. If I close my eyes now, I can feel the joy running through my veins and the void being filled with so much excitement. I had definitely experienced that feeling before but back then, I was not open to receiving it and drama always ruined the show.

It took me a while to understand that joy is accessible to anyone and not only to certain people. We are often blind to it, disregard it or expect it to feel so intense that we fail to actually notice it in the smallest everyday things. I became blind to it for a long time too.

Joy and I actually became close lovers after that freezing day. I learnt more and more how to master it, recognise it and smell it in the smallest and most spontaneous moments of life. Joy is no longer an exotic, extinct ingredient but a highly accessible one which I enjoy savouring alone or with my loved ones.

DEBORA LUZI

INTUITIVE BUSINESS STRATEGIST, CREATIVE WRITER, AND SPEAKER

deboraluzi.com

Debora Luzi is an intuitive business strategist specializing in client attraction. Debora combines strategy and intuition in order to help entrepreneurs show up boldly and authentically, with their truest voice.

Debora is the founder of a supportive and educational online community, 'The Writing Academy for Entrepreneurs" aimed at helping entrepreneurs unleash their writing genius, and selling through their content.

Debora is also the founder of The Women Who Dare to Desire conference, a live centre stage for visionaries women who are ready to inspire the world.

Debora is also a mother to three gorgeous boys and a lover of salsa dancing.

JOY SOUFFLÉ

5 Deep Breaths in Nature

A Handful of Gratitude

A Pinch of Worthiness

A Sprinkle of Commitment

2 Cups of Elevated Emotions

- Emma Gosling -

MAKING LIFE EXTRAORDINARY

A few years back, I had no time for joy. To be honest, I never gave it a lot of thought. I had joyful moments but they seemed to be at the mercy of my external environment. They were fleeting and I was in the habit of leaving joy to chance. If the right ingredients, the right people or the right conditions were not present, then joy was simply not available to me. There were lots of 'ifs' and 'whens' that controlled whether joy would be on the menu or not. 'If business is going well, when I reach my income goals, if I manage to get a full nights' sleep without being woken up'. I was overwhelmed by the trials of running a business and being a mum to a young child. It was exhausting and I was setting myself up for disappointment, allowing my feelings to be controlled by external factors.

After becoming a mum, I started my own business because I wanted more freedom. I wanted to get paid for what I loved doing and to spend more time with my family but I found myself in a trap of becoming overwhelmed and overdoing it. I was never very present when I spent time with my son. I found myself consumed by emails I needed to write, consultations I hoped my husband would be home in time for so he could do bedtime, the social media posts I should be creating. The fear of not having the freedom to do these things was manifesting despite my best efforts. Joy was thin on the ground.

I think many women grow up believing that they need to have it all, do it all, be it all and give it all. If we ask for support, we're deemed inadequate. We're supposed to just get our big girl pants on and deal with it. In trying to do so, we end up falling victim to comparison, guilt, fear and unworthiness. These are the absolute thieves of joy. We give the last mouthful of food on our plate to our kids, our last ounce of affection to our partners, the icing on the cake to our work life and we give ourselves the measly scraps. It's no wonder there is so little time for joy.

I remember having riotous fun when I was young and I remember being scolded by adults for being playful when it was deemed inappropriate. When we're children, it's our natural state to feel joyful but through our experiences of life, we lose those states of being. Many of our experiences of joy as children are shamed out of us, so we shut down certain feelings in order to conform and be accepted. As we grow up, our brains are not physically wired to feel an abundance of joy.

It wasn't until I decided to train as a therapist and mindset coach that I realised the root cause of all this overdoing and lack of joy. Once I had cleared and healed the dis-empowering patterns of behaviour and beliefs about myself, my life started to radically transform. There was now more space for joy. I started to make joy a habit in my daily routine, just like scheduling in exercise. Life started to become more balanced. Nowadays, the more I taste joy, the more time I have to enjoy life. The more I enjoy life, the more doors of opportunity open up that are in alignment with my life purpose which then brings even more joy! I love sharing what I know with others because when I experience joy I feel worthy, powerful, confident, capable and fulfilled. Joy is the catalyst to greatness and without it, we can never become who we are meant to be. If we want our children to experience more joy, they will not learn it by watching us struggle with self-doubt, unworthiness and becoming overwhelmed.

If you have a busy life, build in more time for joy to attract balance and abundance into your life. Just like you make time to clean your teeth every day, feeling joy has to become a habit in order for it to become familiar. Because our minds tend to avoid the unfamiliar.

My recipe for joy starts with gratitude. Walking in nature or driving are good times for me to practice this. I think about the things I love in my life and I allow the tingly, warm feelings to build up in my body as I say words of thanks and gratitude in my mind. Then I take a few deep breaths and smile to release endorphins and engage my senses. I try to hold the feeling for as long as I can. This improves my mood and I feel more able to deal with challenging situations when they occur as I've already filled up my reserve of feel-good feelings. I spend 15 minutes a day listening to a personalised meditation that wires my brain with the elevated emotions of joy, love and gratitude for the things I want in my life that I don't yet have. I am also getting better at catching myself when I slip into negativity and turning my focus to something I am grateful for; a warm hug, sunshine or a butterfly fluttering by. It can be the simplest of things. It takes practice and commitment, but it is absolutely possible to relearn how to experience joy consistently. When we cultivate joy, we can heal ourselves mentally, physically and emotionally. We can make life extraordinary for ourselves and our children.

EMMA GOSLING

TRANSFORMATION THERAPIST
MINDSET COACH

feelgoodenough.co.uk

Emma Gosling is a transformational therapist, clinical hypnotherapist, Quantum Life Technique practitioner, speaker and teacher. She specialises in helping women overcome dis-empowering behaviours and their struggles with comparison, self-sabotage, unworthiness and the fear of being visible. She helps them find their voice and their confidence, love themselves more and supercharge their earning power so they can amplify their business success and live a balanced, abundant and purposeful life.

Emma believes when we are free of our past, we can step into our true power. In order to live an extraordinary life, we first need to reach the root cause of the unhelpful beliefs and thought processes that are running our lives and sabotaging our success at a subconscious level. We can then re-frame and rewire our thoughts to be free to create a joyful, successful, abundant life and align ourselves with who we are meant to be.

INSIDE OUT TREATS

One Slightly Petulant Teenage Caterpillar

The Rhythm of a Beautiful Song

Snuffling Hedgehogs

A Strong, Gentle Voice That Prevails in Chaos

Human Beings With Whom To Dance

- Erica Gibbon -

LISTENING FOR A LOST VOICE

Glum is a word that, strangely, brings me joy. The vocal image of a slightly petulant teenage caterpillar kicking around in a puddle on a wet Saturday morning; her friends away, at a loose end, looking for the meaning of life in her boots. The word requires of me a decision. To take action and lose myself in something beautifully creative that triggers intense focus, consuming all boredom. Or to quietly 'be' with other sentient beings; perhaps search out the friendly snails that appear on my path on wet evenings, not looking at all glum but somehow also waiting for something to happen. Because glum is a barometer of my emotion. Resonance with its' sound brings focus to my mind, a smile to my face and a gleam of mischief to my eye. If I don't resonate with it, I need a different way to grow – permission to allow whatever emotions come up to be processed without reference to time or space; to suffer without becoming the pain; to be an observer - a human being rather than a human doing; to expose myself to fear without being frightened. Glum, for me, connotes compassion, patience and humour, things that help me decide who to be in that moment. It is a good word indeed.

Resonance, I know what it means yet I can't explain it. So I revert to my dictionary, reviving a beautiful memory of autumn evenings as a child, coached to find the correct order of letters-in-my-words and of words-in-my-sentences using the tatty red dictionary in the kitchen cupboard next to the recipe books. Little did I know then that I would come to earn my living using words and recipes to help people find their own joy.

Dictionary located, I read that resonance is 'the sound an object produces when it vibrates at the same speed as another object'. You feel it, rather than hear it. I have forever recognised a vibration deep in my chest when I feel completely in tune with the source of my attention, something akin to a silent, primeval conversation I recognise as joy. It crescendos in me with the chirrup of a bird cajoling me to get out of bed to come and play; the vastness of the sea I drink in on an afternoon break; the intricacy of patchwork fields laid out below me on an Alpine climb; the hypnotic rhythm of a song that compels me to dance; the beating heart of another human being, whether family, friend or stranger.

A second definition of resonance I read is 'a deep, clear sound'. How much I would have loved to own something like that when I was young! In the company of strangers my voice would retreat inside my head, crashing and banging around in chaos as I searched for something worthy to say. Whilst enthralled by people, it seemed to me I might be forever incapable of communicating with them.

And then came my first, very practical lesson in voice. My grandmother shared my bedroom each winter when she came to stay. One morning I found her unable to move, understand or speak. She was given twenty-four hours to live. The family was called and we waited. Eventually they went home with no need to return. My mum was a nurse and I witnessed her strong, gentle dedication administering nourishing soups, tender care and determined encouragement. My grandmother gradually became able to move her fingers, hands, arms, sit up in bed, recognise herself in the mirror, smile, eat, laugh, walk. And talk. A year later she boarded a plane to her homeland without any companion, not even a walking stick. To me as a young teenager, recovery, transformation and defying the odds was the natural order of things. Challenges were to be faced with hope and setbacks accepted as education.

Years later I was called to my father's bedside with little hope of getting there in time. I took hold of his hand, felt a gentle squeeze returned and knew things would be ok. We had six years together after that, watching snuffling hedgehogs, picking blackberries, and recognising the joy in everything small. We helped my dad find his voice when he couldn't find his words, we laughed a lot and it was magical.

Without realising how empowering my unconscious believes had become, I began the adventure of finding my own voice. I trained as an accountant and learned to ask questions. I became a lecturer and learned to have faith in my answers. I travelled and learned to speak in foreign languages – a little - and to listen in foreign cultures. I felt competent communicating with the world but I forgot how to communicate with myself; I'd given away or destroyed all my emotional and physical reserves. When life threw me hand grenades, as is its want, I was completely floored.

But I knew what recovery looked like. So I began to copy it for myself. In following the process a third time I studied in earnest what was much later to become my new career, my new voice and my new joy.

Fifteen years later and I'm preparing to give a lecture to my first year nutrition students. As the time draws near I start to feel butterflies. The old me would have scrambled for books, papers, facts, and figures. The new me wonders what colours the butterflies are and how my students may be feeling. What journey of theirs has led to the crossing of our paths? I feel privileged when strangers trust me enough to allow me into their lives, and I am lucky to have been given a window into many different ways of 'being'.

Window is another great word. It offers me a choice; to look inside and be still, attentive to the voice of my soul. Or to reach out and resume my adventures on this planet with other sentient beings who, just like me, want to be happy. Joy for me is the freedom to choose and the opportunity to do both, I'm encouraged by the piercing night stars that remind me how minuscule I am, how infinitesimally small my troubles and adventures, but how my energy may also be able to travel through time and space to encourage others in their search for more joy.

ERICA GIBBON

NUTRITIONAL THERAPIST AND COACH

lindentreehealth.co.uk

Erica works with 1 to 1 clients from her clinic, Linden Tree Health. She also co-runs Feel Great Formula, providing group retreats for women who want to improve their happiness and health, via education, experience and peer support.

She uses Nutritional Therapy and Functional Medicine to help her clients unpick how food, lifestyle, environmental exposure, relationships and emotions, change, biochemistry and contribute to wellness and disease.

She believes the key to a happy life is to support optimum long-term mental and physical health and is passionate about helping her clients do this via great tasting food, mindset change, building healthy relationships, connecting with the natural world and, when appropriate, using heart rate variability feedback, FAR infrared therapy, neuro-linguistic programming, hypnosis and reiki.

She partners with a variety of other specialists to enable clients to access integrative care and consistent advice.

SPRINKLES OF JOY ICING

Cup of Acceptance, Packed Tight

½ Cup Power of Choice, Softened

¼ Cup Sprinkles of Self Love

A Dash of Meditation (a little goes a long way)

1 Bowl of Kindness

- Hicunni Chandler -

FREE TO EMBODY

I was always looking for outside things to bring me joy. It was a new pair of shoes or a new purse. It was this hidden treasure that could only be uncovered if I really searched for it.

All along, the joy I was seeking was already inside of me. I just had to peel back the layers of indecision, guilt, imposter syndrome, resentment, failures and unresolved conflict. I made peace with those things, letting them go through meditation. I accepted the gifts I have been given and learned how to cultivate them. I choose to love myself with all the hiccups and mishaps over the years. I learnt to embody who I am and be free to express all of me. I now exude joy!

In 1979, a gift of love was born. That's me! Hicunni (Hi Key Knee) actually means a gift of love. I grew up as a shy, thin little girl who loved great food and hid behind her bifocal glasses. I had a poor self image. I felt like an ugly duckling who would never turn into a swan. I've always been really thin and where I lived, being thin was looked down upon. You had to have curves. I was always told that I was too skinny and that I needed to eat.

It wasn't that I didn't eat. I've always been a foodie. However, it didn't matter how much food I ate, I couldn't gain weight. I tried all of the suggestions that people gave me because I wasn't happy with my body or comfortable in my own skin. I tried to be what people wanted me to be.

In addition, as a teenager I felt that I needed to overeat, that somehow if I did that my body might change. As I entered my adult years, I started to examine myself and realized that my weight gaining method wasn't working. Fast forward to being married with kids and it was the least of my worries, especially after finding out that my son had food allergies! A few years later, I found out that I needed to have my gallbladder taken out. I believe the years spent researching what to feed our son prepared me for my toxic gallbladder.

I knew that I wasn't feeding my body what it needed and that contributed to my gallbladder and digestion challenges. My determination kicked in to uncover how the body functions and how to better care for my body in general. Even dealing with my children and their food allergies (later my daughter showed sensitivities) caused me to really want to share tips and strategies to help others on their eating journey. I tried a more therapeutic approach to eating and was able to keep my gallbladder. I felt amazing! I even gained back the weight I lost after a month of my body detoxing. My sister started calling me Google because I became the go to person for the latest food research and good eats.

Finding my foodie freedom continued while I studied for my certification in Eating Psychology and Mind Body Nutrition. Connecting with like-minded individuals was the accountability that I needed to move forward and help others. As I learned how to coach clients, I realized that I had become so militant in my eating. I learned from the founder of the institute that 'what we eat is only half the story, the other half is who we are as eaters.' That statement truly started to resonate with me. I slowly began to see myself as more than what I was eating and more than what I looked like. Self-love added beauty and freedom to my journey and my foodie chronicle.

No more looking at my body as not measuring up or lacking

confidence in building my business online. I chose to live and rewrite my nutritional lifestyle. Throughout my entire journey of self-love and acceptance, the one thing that I believe gave me the perseverance to move forward was meditation. A little goes a long way and with that little ingredient, it has made all the difference to me tuning into who I am and learning to embody joy.

I have been on a mission to share my food story with women, what I call A Foodie Chronicle, to encourage and show them how to find freedom with food and their bodies. I do this by incorporating meditation and mindfulness practices, two things which have been my sustaining grace over the last few years.

As a certified Mind Body Eating Coach, I offer one-on-one coaching and my signature group coaching program, Self Care Mystics. The group connects women who are on a journey to freedom, to embodying self love and to connecting with their higher self. It teaches them to choose to accept life, themselves and the cards they have been dealt, all the while maximizing their self-love. I have learned that this draws more positivity. We are uniting together on our journey of self-love, connecting with our higher selves and being free to embody joy. I invite you on this journey. You too can experience more joy and freedom through food and the body. So grab your smoothie or cup of tea and join the conversation.

HICUNNI CHANDLER

CERTIFIED MIND BODY EATING COACH

hicunnichandler.com

*Hicunni Chandler is a wife and home-schooling mum of two.
A foodie at heart, Hicunni has been helping people with food
allergies, weight loss, body image, meal planning and other
eating challenges for over a decade.*

*Discovering her own journey of self-love and embracing her most
authentic self, she began encouraging women to step out, look
within and discover what truly makes them happy to create
joy in their lives.*

*As a certified Mind Body Eating Coach, she helps women learn
how to love their bodies so that they can find the tools to create
the life they want. Hicunni believes that ;
'only you can be the change that you want to see'. She shares
what she calls 'A Foodie Chronicle', a personal journey of self-love
and travel, inviting you to let go of what no longer serves you and
chose to embrace who you are meant to be.*

COLOUR YOUR LIFE BEAUTIFUL

1 Cup of Living and Working Authentically

A Pinch of Passion

3 Portions of Vulnerability

A Scoop of Attracting New People Into Your Life

5 Portions of Patience

A Helping of Losing Friends Along The Way

*A Dash of Deepening Relationships
With The Ones That Stay*

2 Tbsps of Fun and Enjoying Life To The Fullest

- Jeanne Anette Heinzer-Hiemer -

LIVING YOUR
BEST LIFE ABROAD

I am joyful and grateful for all the good that happens in my life. It gives me joy to share ideas and experiences whether on planes, trains or over Skype. Joy is in my heart the moment others dare to share their lives with me during spontaneous social media discussions or allow me to move them into a lighter space with more clarity. Fear stands for 'false evidence appearing real'. Fear has no power over us unless we allow it to. I choose FUNWAS instead of FEAR, meaning 'Full unlimited normality with a smile.'

The true essence of who we are is joy and the endless abundance that goes with it. Although sometimes difficult, it is possible to sense joy and peacefulness when others try to hurt or ignore you. This is something I learned in my forties. I had arrived in New York City with my two small children. Far from home and with my husband travelling internationally, I felt joy missing in my life. I was unable to be the mother I wanted to be and found myself attending a seminar on Inner Bonding delivered by Dr Margaret Paul in California which allowed me to discover the 'Inner Child Concept'. You simply stay in a safe and centred place where your inner child can be protected by a higher guidance.

When I feel sad or unrested, I take a breath and ask myself what is going on below the surface of the water? How can I bring joy to my inner child? After checking in with myself, I take loving action to move from pain to joy. In the beginning, this process took some time. It now happens on its own.

I was brought up in a household controlled by a strict civil servant with strong Catholic values. I was constantly told that I wasn't good enough and what I wanted was not reasonable. I left my strict German life 30 years ago and moved from Hanover to Paris, the city of my dreams. Changing countries is what my inner child loves and enjoys. Having worked in eight countries and four continents, I am a lifelong student of the art of saying goodbye to a place and the art of setting up a new home from scratch and caring for my children while moving through culture shock. Add the art of maintaining a happy marriage and the art of establishing a new career and you have a handful of arts, all carried out in the most joyful way.

Doing what I used to enjoy as a child or teenager brings joy to my life, things such as painting, drawing, decorating a new space, speaking French and even dressing up as a princess. At age 50, I started sculpting and felt a complete flow of energy. It became an experience of total satisfaction and relaxation. I feel the same way when I am teaching and training people, opening other people's world or expanding an existing world.

I also experience joyful and peaceful moments when I am in Africa. The continent grabbed my heart with a Draconian power, a witch that cast a spell I could not escape. I landed in Casablanca, Morocco in October 2016. I didn't know what would happen in the next 18 months, how my trip to the colourful paradise of 1001 nights would grab my heart with all its might. How it would turn it around, pull it out and leave me as a different person dancing the night away in fancy beach clubs on the Atlantic Ocean only a few hours from the strait of Gibraltar.

I fell in love with this incomplete imperfect place. The shabbiness of it and the friendliness of the Muslim population captured and conquered my heart. I discovered tagine, mint tea, couscous and Islam, the way I had discovered Paris 25 years before. My bodyguard, driver, assistant and friend Simo is a young and handsome Muslim man, a singer and model living in the poorest area in the slums of Casablanca. I met Simo during my first visit when I was intending to check out Morocco as a potential family destination.

I eventually decided to buy a luxury apartment on the ocean next to the Four Seasons Hotel in Marrakech, my favourite hotel chain. I had the glorious task of furnishing this huge apartment while being a single mum in Basel and preparing for my future family life in Johannesburg, South Africa. I decorated my apartment on the beach in gold and black, buying one colourful Moroccan royal outfit after the other and wearing new clothes in luxury hotels.

Within three years I must have visited Marrakech 40 times. Choosing a different luxury riad each time, drinking Moroccan wine on rooftop terraces and indulging in Moroccan jewellery. I feel happy and content in a simple and smoky Shisha bar in a shabby side street or speaking French endlessly with warm and welcoming Muslims. Joy at its peak.

One day Simo (who many think is my husband which is flattering as he is 20 years younger than me) will drive me in a long black limousine to the third biggest mosque in the world right on the waterfront. However for the time being, a shabby black Peugeot has to fulfil this role. My dream life continues, followed by a luxurious apartment in Paris to close my life circle.

JEANNE ANETTE HEINZER-HIEMER

LICENCED CAREER COUNSELOR
MASTER INSEAD CHANGE MANAGEMENT

heinzerconsulting.com

Jeanne Heinzer loves boosting the careers of aspiring young to mid-career professionals by developing their potential to achieve results and international success. She provides them with access to an international network and a vision and strategy for a successful and satisfying personal and professional life.

She guides professionals through profound personal, work and organisational change, supporting their potential, transition and leadership development. She also enables global employees to continue their international career at a top level. She assists them to identify new job opportunities and deal with challenges while leading, managing and motivating a foreign workforce to achieve top performance and corporate success in a responsible, ethical and joyful way.

Jeanne draws upon her background in organisational and clinical psychology and 30 years of international work experience to provide tailor made Change Management, Communication and Career Development Programmes for individuals, couples and corporate teams who wish to go global in an ethical way.

Abundant thinking base

A Sprinkle of 'I am enough'

Copious amounts of Gratitude

A Topping of Spiritual Practice and Meditation

Icing of Faith and Manifestation

- Jelena Radonjic -

ORIENTATION OF THE HEART

'No matter what you do in life, whether you sell vegetables at the market, work as a doctor or teach, do it with honesty and integrity. All work is good work and deserves appreciation if done with dedication, purpose and honesty'. When I was seven, my mother's words impressed upon me the importance of serving others and working with honesty and integrity.

As a child I was industrious and liked to study. My curiosity grew as I matured and I began to explore the works of Erich Fromm, Carl Jung, Paolo Coelho and the Eastern philosophies. At 18, I took up transcendental meditation, which was quite unusual in then-socialist Yugoslavia. I was mesmerised with Zen Buddhism, Japanese Haiku poetry, parts of Bhagavad Gita and anything spiritual I could get my hands on. My search for meaning and the unknowable was incessant, and I was intrigued by what lay beneath.

Attracted to the Far East, I chose to study Japanese alongside English. After four and a half years of hard work, I graduated at the top of my class with a double major. This led to a corporate job in Tokyo, an opportunity that was practically unheard of in 1991 pre-war Yugoslavia. I left on the wings of excitement and anticipation.

My job in recruitment aligned well with my passion for connecting people and serving as a catalyst for work-life fulfilment, which led me to become a career coach many years later. Although I never predicted it, a new chapter of my life began.

I was elated with my new life in Tokyo. My hard work was rewarded with more responsibility and opportunities to travel in Europe and the US. However, the gruelling, energy-sapping 15-hour days and long commute meant my spiritual interests took a back seat. I had to learn to find the right balance between adapting to a very different culture and honouring my own needs.

My faith, confidence and naturally sunny disposition helped me thrive in a challenging, male-dominated environment. Being young, foreign and a woman were the three worst career pitfalls but I embraced it all with gratitude, an essential prerequisite for joy. I had an intuitive feeling that if I offer my best then the best will come back to me. After four years in Tokyo, I transferred to the London office and was quickly promoted to Director of European Operations. Despite approaching life with an open mind and an open heart, pressure was mounting to give everything to my work. I gave up my dream of doing a Masters in London, and I only took a few months maternity leave after having my first son.

In all this 'busy-ness', I had forgotten to take care of myself. I had abandoned my spiritual interests which had always fed my soul and gradually my life started to unravel. Over the years I felt increasingly torn between work and family, feeling unappreciated in both and breeding resentment. The thief of joy.

In the meantime, my country had gone not only through a cruel civil war but Serbia endured the NATO bombing in 1999. I felt there was a black veil covering my eyes and a deep dark hole opening in my heart. There was no joy, just pain and fear for the lives of my parents, friends and relatives who still lived in Belgrade. I took a longer break from work after having my second son and volunteered for a charity supporting orphans in war-ravaged parts of ex-Yugoslavia.

After a divorce, family issues and a lengthy year of cancer treatment, it was as though the universe was asking me to remember who I truly was and to choose joy. I started to wake up. I would sing in the car driving myself to chemotherapy, feeling happy that I was alive and given a chance to live more. I cultivated joy despite everything. Through all of this emotional and mental turmoil, I began to learn to accept and let go. I threw myself into personal development and spiritual work as though my life and my children's lives depended on it – because they did! Through sheer perseverance, faith and an unwavering curiosity to find out what is at the bottom of it all, I survived and started rebuilding my life. I worked tirelessly on myself and gradually managed to put myself in my sovereign space. By doing so, the children found their own place and grounding. Like helpless leaves in a tornado, we started to land as the storm subsided. A sense of relief followed, precariously hanging on to a thin veneer of peace.

I moved from surviving to thriving. I put all my knowledge, experience, passion and drive into launching my career coaching business. Numerous difficulties and traumatic events have opened my heart to compassion and my mind to understanding. Through my spiritual work, my intuition was sharpened. It thrills me to see my clients progress from 'I can't do that' to 'yes, I've done it!" Understanding why we often do things we do not want to, or stop ourselves from doing things we really want to, is so empowering and sharing this with my clients brings me joy. However, my biggest joy is raising awareness in myself and others. With fresh insights we can take inspired action and move towards living a life of purpose, fulfilment and joy.

JELENA RADONJIC

CAREER FULFILMENT COACH

whatwork.co.uk

Jelena is an award-winning Career Fulfilment Coach passionate about helping aspiring professionals thrive in the careers they love. With 25 years in international recruitment and education management, Jelena is a qualified coach and speaker providing unique insights into how recruiters think and how personal coaches work. Her clients have secured roles in Amazon, HSBC, Imperial College, Tottenham Hotspur FC, or set up their own business.

Her motto is Fresh Insights – Inspired Action.

Jelena has also worked with spiritual teachers such as DeMartini and Chopra and infuses love, joy and spirit into her coaching. Passionate about spiritual practice and transformation, she is an avid reader and lifelong learner.

MELTING MOMENTS

1 Female

1 Amazing Outfit

An Assortment of Makeup

1 Mirror

- *Jo Haley* -

IGNITE YOUR REFLECTION

It was 11.45am. I walked into the hotel ready to start another day of work. The reception area was busy with guests coming and going. The lounge was full of shoppers with their morning coffee and the workers were busy having their meetings. I walked into the servery, hung up my stuff and said hello to the rest of the team. It was definitely going to be another busy day. A conference was being held at the hotel and I had been looking after all the participants for the past few days. While they broke for lunch, I went in to clear and tidy the room. It was in this room that my life changed.

Jen, my best friend from college and I had not long been back from travelling the world. We spent an incredible eight months together having the time of our lives, so it was great knowing I had a job in my parents' hotel when I got home. We met so many amazing people, saw so many incredible sights and had the best experiences ever. Being with people was one of my biggest passions. I just loved helping others and making sure that they were always having a good time. I liked knowing that whatever they were doing, they were being looked after and made to feel special. This eventually led me into the world of beauty, makeup, skincare and image.

I was clearing up the coffee cups and straightening up the pads and pens when I saw it. Someone had drawn my necklace, the one I wore every day. On a writing pad, underneath it was the word drink? I had no idea which gentleman had written it but I had a choice of 12! I was very excited walking back to the restaurant. I looked at them all as they were having lunch and I could feel his eyes staring at me. We ended up going out for a drink the next day and before I knew it, our relationship had blossomed and we were living together. After many obstacles and challenges, we eventually moved into his marital home. We had his children living with us and I became a mummy at the age of 21 to a four and three-year-old. Times were tough but I got on with it. However, it all changed one evening when he hit me for the first time. A punch in the face. By this time, my parents had sold up and moved back to our hometown so I had nobody to turn to.

Time went by and so did the beatings, the hurt and the anger. What had I ever done but be there for him and his children? I knew I had to leave but I also knew it wasn't going to be easy. I had nothing left in me. One morning as I was covering up my black eye, I remembered how much I loved the beauty world and how much I had wanted to be a beautician. I began to plan my escape. I moved back in with my parents during the week and went to beauty college. I went 'home' on the weekends so he wouldn't suspect anything, knowing that as soon as the course was finished I'd leave for good. However it was 5 years later that I finally managed to leave - the beatings still continued - you learn to cope. Leaving him was one of the hardest things I've ever done both emotionally and physically, but I was ready for the next stage of my life.

I loved my new life. I had some great friends, I got a job in a department store as a beauty consultant and I also ran the in-house studio for facials. It all felt perfect. I had my own line of customers who I would give makeup and skincare tutorials to so that they too could feel special. I loved it so much that I stayed for seven years. My passion for helping women to feel great about themselves has never left me. We forget how worthy we are and how we mustn't let others bring us down. We should learn to love ourselves and to take pride in our appearance.

I am not a follower of fashion or an 'on-trend' kind of gal but I do like to look nice and feel good about myself so I found myself training to be an image consultant. It was a true eye-opener. Who knew that getting dressed 'correctly' could be so complex? We are creating a work of art when we put on our clothes and at the same time creating optical illusions. There is so much to learn and it gives me huge joy to pass this onto others.

As women, we go through so many transitions in our lives but can lose our identity, self-esteem, confidence and self-worth along the way. Our wardrobes are bursting at the seams but we still have nothing to wear. Our makeup stays the same from day to night, from work to the Christmas party. We just don't know who we are anymore. In my role as The Positive Image Coach, I see women who are deflated. It's my job and passion to show them how great they are and how their body is beautiful just by being uniquely their own. I educate them on how to dress so that they can shine, feel empowered and boost their identity. My aim is to help them establish confidence and reclaim their self-esteem so when they walk out of their front door in the mornings, they feel proud of who they are and walk through life with an all new abundance of joy.

JO HALEY

THE POSITIVE IMAGE COACH

thepositiveimagecoach.co.uk

Jo Haley is The Positive Image Coach. Her attention was drawn to image while working as a makeup artist for a styling company in Hong Kong. She became interested in the way they taught and educated women to understand and work on their body shapes, styles and personalities. She now acts on her lifelong passion to empower women to become their best selves.

16 years ago, Jo trained as an image consultant, earning her Masters in Image Consultancy. She is one of 18 in the world with this accreditation from the Federation of Image Professionals and it is the only recognisable national and international qualification for her profession.

Her attention is not about on-trend fashion but instead about the uniqueness of each woman. She helps ladies to really see and get to know their body shape, their needs, their lifestyle and their desires. Her achievements include her role as an Ambassador for the Body Image Movement, a global movement which helps people truly understand who they are, what they look like and how to embrace it.

STORY SCONES

1 Original Idea

A Few Lessons To Learn

A Pinch of Comedy, Tragedy, Romance or Fantasy

Add a Twist or a Turn

- Jodie and Paris Welton -

CONNECTED SISTERS

Storytelling has earned its place as one of the most important traditions we possess as humans. It crosses culture, race, gender, geographical and age boundaries and is accepted as beneficial from the moment we are born. Stories have the power to improve our situation. We use them to enhance the development of infants with sound, word and language formation. They are used to soothe children and make them feel safe at bedtime while adults use them for entertainment, extended learning or relaxation. Storytelling holds its value through all stages of life; it can teach us tolerance, respect, to love, forgive and generally improve ourselves and our lives. But what if storytelling is more powerful than this? What if telling true stories has the power to shift cultural paradigms, break down social injustices and empower marginalized or disadvantaged populations? Well, my sister and I think that it does. In fact, we are certain that it does. This is our story, a story about storytelling and why we are backing it with all we have got.

We grew up in the eighties in a household where money was sparse and traditional gender roles were not questioned. Our father went to work, our mother looked after the children. We witnessed our extremely capable and intelligent mother leave her career behind in favour of raising four children. Flash forward to the nineties and both my sister and I chose further and higher education. We became the first in our family on either side to attend university. Several jobs later and we noticed our male colleagues excelling quicker in the work place, we noticed we were more outnumbered by our male counterparts the further we climbed in corporate settings and we experienced the #metoo movement first hand. Significant as this all was to us, it sadly isn't remarkable or particularly different to the millions of other working women and what they deal with day to day. We decided to leave 'employment' and set up our own PR agency. We thrived, we worked, we excelled, we travelled, we were our own bosses and we experienced work on our own terms. We developed a taste of what 'work' is like for men – freedom, good pay, benefits, autonomy. It was amazing. It was also temporary.

When we both became mothers, the duality of working at 'work' and working at 'home' became a daily challenge. The expectation for women to work like they don't have children and parent like they don't work was our reality. For the first time in our lives we started thinking about our gender roles seriously. Did we really carry limitations simply because we were born female? Surely not. We had educated ourselves, we had successfully weaved our way through our career paths and we were managing families, staff and a thriving business.

One morning we were on the 5.45am train heading to Waterloo for a work commitment. Before I left the house I had tiptoed around my sleeping family to make my husband and children breakfast and packed lunches and dinner because I knew I was going to be home late. I left the clothes out for the children and wrote reminders for my husband. 'Don't forget PE kit', 'pick up is at 3.30pm' and 'nap time is 1pm, please have snack ready for when she wakes'. We have three children and the reminders are expressions of the mental load I was carrying. I know how hard it can be to get organised in the morning so I always helped out if I had to work by leaving food ready and prepared. So sitting on the quiet train sipping my coffee and checking my email was a welcome moment of calm, even if it was before 6am!

Two men to our left were chatting and grumbling about the early start. They both had food prepared by their wives and one was texting his wife to say thanks for the breakfast she had made him.

'She's probably sleeping. This will wake her up', he joked. 'Easy life, lying in bed with the kids', he went on. The disparity between working mums and working dads suddenly seemed so ridiculous to me that it was almost funny. My sister and I laughed to ourselves. As the years passed we would talk often about life experiences and gender roles. We were fortunate enough to be able to speak to hundreds of women from varying cultures and backgrounds as part of our business and we learned about the diverse challenges faced by these women, some were relatable and work related, many others were not. Nonetheless the common theme throughout was the unique female experience and a story untold. We yearned to help them and future generations. We both have daughters and the quest to help women started to feel personal. Entrepreneurial by nature, both of us devised business ideas. We plotted and schemed what we felt were ground-breaking ideas but none of them stuck. We would call each other excited by a new idea almost every week, only to scrap it and start again a few days later.

Eventually, the simple idea of hearing women tell their stories seemed like the best place to start. We knew that if women would share their truth with us, we would be able to use our skills to share it with other women. In a world that benefits from women being in competition with one another; fighting to get that job (good jobs for women are in short supply), competing to 'get that man' (mass media will have you believe that physical prowess will achieve this), creating the perfect home (also the women's job), bringing up perfect children (yep, women's job also), we wondered about creating unity and connecting women. We wanted to help create a Sisterhood, a safe place where women can share their truth, tell their stories and inspire other women to do the same. We created Connected Sisters to do exactly that. But it's more than this. Storytelling can connect people emotionally to a worldview that shapes values, and true stories have an added benefit because these values are born through lived experiences not just abstract principals. We believe that the female voice needs to be heard now more than ever. Connected Sisters is our contribution to help women connect, empowering women through shared experiences and maybe over time, it will disrupt the gender bias and make things a little better for the girls of tomorrow.

JODIE AND PARIS WELTON

FOUNDERS OF CONNECTED SISTERS
AND CONNECTED PR

connectedsisters.com

Jodie and Paris Welton are sisters and business partners who have successfully run their PR agency Connected PR for over a decade. Having both transitioned into working mothers, their working time became more focused as did their desire to create something that would help other women.

Connected Sisters was born. In an era where information is no longer power, what we need now is wisdom, love and compassion. So they are inviting women to tell their stories and share their wisdom with their sisters all over the world. The media we consume is often set to a male agenda, setting false expectations for the female experience, focusing on all of the things that are "wrong" with us and trying to sell us products to achieve unachievable perfection. They challenge this and through Connected Sisters are telling the truth about the female experience, one story at a time.

Connected Sisters is a safe digital space for truth, a virtual women's circle where we can learn and grow and support one another.

DREAMY LOVE MUFFINS

1 Blanket of Dreams

2 Beautiful Children

1 Gorgeous Hubby

2 Cups of Hugs with Loved Ones

5 Abundance/Wealth Walks

1 Bowl of Laughter

A Pinch of Journalling

- Julie Sylvia Kalungi -

THE WEALTH WITHIN

Every day I choose joy and dreams.

Since I was a child living in Uganda, I have found joy in the simplest of things. My dad died when I was just four years old, leaving my teenage mother alone. I was soon shipped off to my uncle's home to be raised and have a better chance in life.

I was usually left under the eye of the housemaid who was quick to smack me for anything she felt I was doing wrong. She made me clean dishes, pots and pans twice my size. I swept a compound half an acre big and mopped the massive five-bedroom home daily. By the age of six, I was an expert daydreamer. My dreams were an escape from reality and a source of pure joy.

I often wondered what my four cousins were doing while I worked so hard to keep the house clean and tidy. When I asked, I was smacked so I learned to close my mouth and get on with my chores. Apart from my daydreams, I found escape and joy in a huge old mango tree in the compound. I would climb the tree to hide from the housemaid but also to munch on the juicy, ripe or tangy green fruit and daydream about my mum and dad. I'd close my eyes and dream of a life in a land filled with fluffy white sugar, beautiful cottages and children playing. I picked these particular images from cards I saw the first Christmas with my uncle. Whatever life threw my way, I would escape up the tree and dream of Sugar Land.

My first true experience of this childhood Sugar Land was during my early 20's while studying for a Masters in Law in Uganda and I visited UK. At the time, the UK had an unprecedented cold spring with snow and gale force winds through the whole month of April. The city was covered in that fluffy white sugar I once imagined and in my freezing discomfort, I was transported right back up that mango tree where I felt safe and at home. I didn't like the cold weather in the UK but five years later, after my Masters was finished and I had returned home to Uganda, I came back to England with my husband and our baby to live.

Beginning a life in the UK with my family was a chance to manifest the blanket of warmth and hope I felt so often in the mango tree of my youth. In 2010, I had walked away from an average job in construction. Together with my husband's income, we were an average middle-class family. To someone looking in, we were okay. Two cars, a home in the suburbs, two healthy children and a vacation twice a year. What was not to love? However, we had just endured 18 months of being homeless after a flood took our home the year before and things were taking their toll.

I felt suffocated both at work and at home. I felt like I was living a lie. Two years of throwing a giant pity party and praying for a miracle, I was introduced to direct selling and was reminded of all the skills I already possessed. I discovered that I had the business admin and personal branding knowledge that others were praying for. It was a wake-up call to show up and serve and I began coaching others in business strategy. I just knew I had a story in me so I published my first book, Journey Without Limits and things began to look up.

I wasn't hugged much as a child but I love to hug and be hugged. My husband is a hugger too. We love a group hug. For me a family hug on a Caribbean beach is my cup overflowing. We even e-Hug when any one of us is away travelling. To activate our joy and increase abundance in our lives, we do nature walks as a family. When the children were little, we'd go rambling in Wales. It was all we could afford at the time. We laughed lots as our children noticed the abundant nature around them, things my husband and I grew up around and took for granted. Sheep, chickens, cows, horses, butterflies and a variety of plants. We learned to expand our abundance and release work stress through being in nature and laughing. Laughter is indeed our natural expression of joy. It's the best medicine.

Over the past six years, we have followed John Maxwell and other amazing coaches who have opened our eyes to nature thriving all around us. The plants, grass, trees, wind, sky and birds. We acknowledge the fact that this is our universe. We manifested Sugar Land together so we can just as easily manifest anything. Now our children have grown, my husband and I still take our abundance walks every weekend. These walks give us a chance to talk about our life, children, relationship, work, business and community. We give ourselves the opportunity to brainstorm and to work through challenges together. We always return home feeling fresher, clearer, usually quite sweaty and laughing our heads off.

Another thing that keeps me sane, focused, growing and revisiting every joyous moment in my life is journalling. So much so, that I created a 2-in-1 journal and 90-day planner called The Winning Planner, a resource for those juggling both a personal life and business life

As somebody once said, 'life is lived in moments and mine are captured in minute details every blessed day'. Capturing my life into a journal helped me overcome trauma, depression and all of life's little setbacks. The abundance walks, journalling, meditating and praying, being open to learning every day and knowing that I have always been blessed are my joy.

JULIE SYLVIA KALUNGI

BUSINESS TRANSFORMATIONAL STRATEGIST AND COACH

kalungigroup.com

Julie Sylvia Kalungi was born in Uganda and moved to the United Kingdom with her daughter and husband at 28 years old. In Uganda, she was a legal practitioner yet she came from much humbler beginnings.

In the UK, she started working as a carer and eventually became a customer services manager in housing. Today, she is a leading pinterest strategist, celebrated blogger and business transformational strategist for entrepreneurs in the Afro/European community. She trains marketers and business owners, helping them to organize, scale and build a business that serves their lifestyle. She is a professional speaker and a passionate Christian. Described by many of her clients as a giving, inspirational mentor and coach, Julie inspires her clients to take action, helping them to leverage the online space, adopt a new mindset and embrace digital techniques to expand their reach.

She is a wife, mother of two, a community leader and a fierce family woman, working from home while serving her family's needs.

A BOWL OF WELLBEING

A Palm-sized Amount of High Quality Protein

A Bunch of Rainbow Vegetables

1-3 Tbsps of High Quality Fats

3 Pleasurable Exercise Sessions

20 Minutes of Meditation

A Daily Dose of Sunshine and Fresh Air

- Laura Butler -

THE PLEASURABLE PATH TO TRUE HEALTH

Through bleary eyes, I looked at the clock to the side of the bed. I could just make out the time. 4.59am. The tug on my arm grew stronger. 'Up Mummy, up Mummy' came the tiny voice, urging me onto my feet and down the stairs, still half asleep. The children were boundless balls of fun regardless of the early hour. They only noticed my sleep deprived state when I was grumpy and short with them, fumbling for coffee. Envious of their energy and alertness, I knew how the day was going to go. My ground-hog day of starting on the back foot and not feeling like I was succeeding in any area of my life - family, work, relationships or health.

I didn't know I was setting myself up for failure by just the things I was fuelling my body with. It was a daily cycle of starting the day with multiple coffees to try and feel human and grabbing whatever food was on hand throughout the day. Usually this would be something sugary or stodgy to glean a feeling of comfort or momentary satisfaction and relief from the struggles of the day. More coffee, rushed meals, always eating but never satiated. I was always on the go with kids, work and family. I was always doing and everyone else came first from dawn to dusk. After the kid's bedtimes, I would collapse with a list as long as my arm of chores but it was straight to opening emails and catching up on client work. More snacks and wine were my evening solution. I would mindlessly eat my emotions, looking for that instant gratification. I was eating my emotions to try and fill the void. Inevitably, it always ended with feelings of guilt and regret when I felt the tightness of my jeans. The guilt, oh the guilt! Whatever I did and whoever I did it for, the guilt was crushing in every area.

I felt overwhelmed daily. The pressures of motherhood and the needs of two young children were exhausting enough. Couple that with running a successful business and working late into the night. The effects of not making my health and wellbeing a priority were becoming obvious. My low mood and constant stressed state were making me snappy and irritable to those I loved. I was missing valuable moments with the children by not being present or at my best. My confidence was waning because I wasn't able to regain my pre-baby figure. My zest for life was diminishing so rapidly, I barely knew who I was anymore. I knew I wanted the cycle to stop but I didn't know how to break it. I didn't know I had the power to change my whole life with a few simple tweaks. I didn't know there was another way.

Skip forward to the present day and my days couldn't be more different! I started my journey of transformation by making the decision to serve others. I wasn't sure how but I was determined to build on my coaching qualifications and revisit a passion of mine from a young age - health and wellbeing. You would think that adding a new qualification and learning journey would add to the stress of my already pressured life but the opposite happened.

I finished my training as a health and habit change coach with a deep responsibility to teach others what I now knew. I felt like I was in possession of some mythical treasure such was the value I placed on these new learned tools. I looked around at friends and family who all had similar struggles to my previous self and made a vow that I would help them in any way I could. The strongest calling was to support my fellow modern day mums, these superwomen who are raising the next generation under a pile of pressures and responsibilities with little to no help to prevent burning out and becoming overwhelmed.

When I think back to where I was three years ago, I so desperately want to reach out to the old me and give struggling Laura a hug. I want to whisper all the secrets I have learned about health to her, show her that there is another way, a more joyful and fulfilling way. You can have balance, good health, mental wellbeing, run a successful business and be a great, present mum too. You just need to be brave enough to take on the journey of self-discovery, break the loop of painful habits, get curious, dig deep, listen to your body and your intuition and learn. The definition of insanity is doing the same thing over and over and expecting a different result.

This journey can be fun and enjoyable if you allow it to be. Don't believe the diet hype that keeps you trapped in the yo-yo diet cycle. You can be fit, healthy and at optimum weight without deprivation, starvation or militant exercise. It really can be pleasurable! It's in the trial and error that the magic happens. It won't be a straight road, it's not an exact science and you are going to have to break old habits that feel like comfortable old slippers (but they have holes in and no longer serve a purpose). Get ready to put on new ones that may take a little time to wear in.

You can't do it alone. Support, accountability, love and a kind, respectful internal dialogue with yourself will get you through. Remember to connect regularly to your motivation and reason for change. The fierce desire to be a well rounded role model to your children will push you on to succeed in all these areas.

I now regularly take stock and check in with my 'Wheel of Life' tool I use with all my clients. I make sure my boundaries and new baselines haven't slipped, that each bucket on my wheel of life is kept full and is nourishing me. While physical nourishment is essential, it is not the whole picture. It is the nourishment of all the areas in our lives that ultimately lead to our quality of wellbeing.

Nourishment brought joy to my life. When we are properly nourished there is no place for stress, cravings, illness, worry and the other niggling ailments of life that like to keep us down. When we approach our health and wellbeing as a pleasurable journey, we allow joy to enter.

LAURA BUTLER

LIFESTYLE INTERVENTION CONSULTANT

laurabutlercoaching.co.uk

Laura Butler is a Health and Habit Change Coach. She is the founder of the welLBe Transformation Systems and Women's Health Transformation Academy.

Laura is dedicated to health and wellness. She serves businesses and organisations across the UK and helps ambitious, entrepreneurial and career driven women globally. Laura provides 1-2-1 sessions, group workshops and blended approaches in her profound coaching programmes for her corporate and private practise. She inspires her clients to harness the power to become the best version of themselves. She inspires them to look good and feel good inside and out and create the life they dream of.

She simplifies the approach to health and wellness while creating fast results without deprivation or militant exercise. Using cutting edge neuroscience to re-wire thought patterns, a strong support and accountability system alongside transformational health and habit change coaching techniques, Laura is a specialist in her field and helps her clients make changes that last.

A JOYOUS DAY

1 Bunch of Happy People

1 Bunch of Beautiful Horses

1 Long Nature Trail

A Dash of Wildlife

Optional: Sunshiny Day with a Sprinkle of Clouds

- Lisa Houston -

IN AN INSTANT

Why am I telling you my story? My hope is that I can make a difference in someone else's life by sharing how I learned to overcome my own trauma and live a fulfilling life. I truly believe that each one of us has great potential to overcome anything as long as we believe in ourselves. No matter what anyone tells you, it's really up to you to determine what direction your life takes. You can believe what others say and give up, or you can decide to take charge of your own destiny. You always have a choice. You are not a victim of your circumstances - unless you choose to be. Your past does not determine your future - unless you choose to let it. You are not who or what other people say or believe you are - unless you choose to accept their beliefs and labels.

Did you ever think your life could drastically change in an instant? One sunny spring day when I was feeling happy and thinking life was pretty perfect, my life changed in an instant. I had a beautiful family that I loved, I had a great job and I had recently adopted a rescue horse. It was a splendid day out at the barn, my happy place, and I was filled with joy riding my dream horse. But in an instant I found myself slammed to the ground in excruciating pain, unable to stand or walk. Lying on the ground, I looked up and saw my horse standing over me. What had just happened?

A few hours later, my husband, daughter and I fervently awaited the results from the x-rays and other tests in the emergency room. The news we received would forever impact my entire life and my family. Previously I had been a happy, healthy wife and mother, and now we were all hit with the profound weight of this unimaginable news. While I was sitting in that wheelchair listening to the doctors saying that they weren't sure whether I would walk again, much less ride my horse again, I was in shock, angry and full of fear. My whole world had been turned upside down. How would this affect my active lifestyle and my family's life together? My job? My health?

At that moment I knew I had a decision to make. I realized that I could accept what the doctors said, consequently staying stuck and broken in that wheelchair for the rest of my life, gripping onto fear, rooted in anger, and feeling sorry for myself. Or I could choose to face my fears and believe in my own inner strength. I could not foresee a future unable to walk or ride my horse. I would not accept it. I believed in my heart that I would walk again and eventually ride my horse again. Riding horses was my passion, my joy and an amazing sense of freedom, almost like flying. How could I live my life without this passion that brought me so much happiness? The very thought of losing such a big part of my life drove me to work even harder to regain my health and happiness. Although it wasn't an easy journey, through various surgeries and physical therapy, I learned how to harness belief in myself and lean on the support of my family and friends.

I had a goal to be walking and riding my horse again, so I put everything I had into accomplishing it. I had no idea how long it would take for me to be able to walk again or get back on my horse. I just knew I had to do it. Walking was painful and awkward; however, I realized that I could sit on my horse and ride with minimal pain. I have always loved hiking and being outside in nature. I found that when I was riding in the wooded trails, my horse could be my legs. I could ride for miles on the magnificent trails, enjoying the outdoors with my horse, feeling free and full of joy. Even if I couldn't walk very far, I could ride. Riding my horse again sparked self-confidence and belief in myself. Eventually I would walk again, slowly and painfully at first but each day taking steps to move forward towards my goal.

As I started feeling better and better, I got involved in other activities. A friend asked me if I could help with a local non-profit organization that provided equine therapy for veterans. Though I really didn't know much about helping veterans, I did know something about horses, so I was happy to volunteer my time. Much to my surprise, I bonded with the veterans, most of whom had severe injuries. I was humbled by their perseverance and annoyed that I had felt sorry for myself in my situation, knowing what some of those veterans had gone through. This experience would forever change my life. That is when I knew that sharing my own experiences and knowledge could really help others find the strength and belief to keep moving forward and overcome the challenging circumstances and conditions in their lives.

As an individual, you can choose to believe in what others say, or you can choose to eradicate those beliefs, overwrite them in your mind and introduce positive beliefs that can truly shift your thinking. You always have a choice, every moment of your life, to decide how you feel about or react to a situation. Only you can make the decision to experience happiness and joy in your life.

LISA HOUSTON

FOUNDER OF ZENCOURAGEMENT COACHING AND TRAUMA RECOVERY EXPERT

zencouragementcoaching.com

Lisa Houston discovered her passion for helping people after a traumatic horseback-riding accident. During her recovery, Lisa began volunteering at an equine therapy organization for disabled veterans. She not only experienced incredible encouragement and hope from spending time with veterans and volunteers but also learned to be humble and love her life just as it was.

In 2016, Lisa was interviewed by Cheryl Ginnings, radio host of Courage2Overcome about how she rose above her physical disabilities from the accident, built up her coaching skills and began sharing her experiences to help others facing trauma or injuries.

As a certified life coach, Lisa works with organizations and individual clients, supporting and empowering them to establish positive beliefs, tap into their inner power and shift their energy towards reaching their highest potential, thus effectively achieving their results in finding richer and more fulfilling lives. Lisa's transformational coaching techniques and heart-centred style provides her clients with the tools to create life-altering outcomes.

SELF-LOVE CHOCOLATE FONDANT

1 Tbsp of Self-Compassion

2 Cubes of Forgiveness

100ml of Physical Activity

2 Tbsps of Spontaneity

1 Pinch of Gratitude

2 Tbsps of Peace of Mind

A Cup of Integrity and Self Respect

- Marisabelle Bonnici -

THE CONFIDENCE CROWN

In 2017, I was the heaviest I have ever been. I weighed 139kg and realised that if I was to keep on this way, I was not going to live for very long. There is only so much abuse a body can take! I had been binging, restricting and yo-yo dieting for over twenty years. I even had a phase at university where I lost over 30kg in a couple of months by literally refusing to eat anything. Two and a half years ago, I decided it was time for a change. I could not keep feeling miserable about myself and my life any longer. I started by working on myself. I learnt to love myself to the point of waking up every morning with a heart overflowing with gratitude for all I had in my life. My main aim for several months was to love myself unconditionally - quirks, flaws, hard head, thick thighs and all, to love myself the way I hoped someone else would some day love me. I loved fiercely and was unafraid to show it. But this story didn't start overnight; it's been a long time in the making.

If you grew up anything like me, you grew up hearing the phrases "finish your meal!" or "clean your plate!" My parents and grandparents would often make me feel guilty for leaving food on my plate. I grew up thinking you had to finish your entire plate, even when you were full. I eventually ended up turning to food as a way of comfort in times of stress, anxiety and loneliness. I was severely bullied at school for being taller and bigger than the other girls. In actual fact, I was not overweight. I was just built differently. I was also bullied for loving books and playing an instrument that was not the norm – the piano accordion. My refuge at the time was the library and my music but I was bullied so much about both that I ended up turning to food to help me. The bullying continued until I was around sixteen and by then, my self-esteem was already severely damaged. Food was my refuge. It was the one thing that made me feel good about myself. Today, I know that certain foods boost serotonin levels and have an antidepressant effect. The effects of food on the mind are similar to strong drugs. Certain foods cause the release of feel good hormones like GABA, serotonin and endorphins. This high is what I needed to help me through tough times. Over the years, a relationship with a narcissist and misogynist also left my self-esteem damaged. For a long time, I believed that my worth was tied to my weight. I used to put myself down and refuse to go out on dates as I felt I was too unattractive and overweight to love.

On a cold and rainy February day in 2017, a dear friend asked me, "Belle, are you happy with who you are?" I had no answer to this question. For several minutes I sat in silence. Not because I didn't know the answer but rather because I knew it instantly. I remember shaking my head, not being able to utter any sound as warm tears rolled down my eyes.

I did not like myself or my negative head-space. I certainly did not love myself. And it was my fault. I had negative thoughts and attracted negative energy and people. I kept putting myself last, making choices to care for others before myself. Sometimes it's so easy to give all your care and love to others and not feed yourself any of that same love given away. Many people feel that self-love can be selfish but it most definitely is NOT! Take care of your body, mind and soul. I do this every day. I start my mornings with yoga and meditation and plan to nourish my body with the right foods in advance every weekend. I work out at the end of all my days. I devote some time to myself every day.

I have stopped viewing yoga as a fitness tool or a means to lose weight. I am using it as a powerful vehicle for self-exploration. It is the ultimate display of self-love and I use it to practice mindfulness. A great butt and toned tummy–should they appear one day–would simply be a side effect of choosing myself. Choosing myself is the best choice I have ever made in my life. I have also learnt to forgive myself. We are our own worst critics and I spent so many years using negative talk to describe myself. We are not perfect beings. We need to love ourselves more for those imperfections, accept them, forgive ourselves and keep falling in love with ourselves every day. I have learnt to embrace who I am. My relationship with myself is built on solid foundations and positive thoughts.

On my journey to self-love, I have completely eliminated toxic people from my life. I surround myself with positive and optimistic people who will only keep on nourishing my mind and soul. I keep challenging myself every day, developing my mind through books and learning and developing my body and physical strength through regular workouts. All of these things have led me to the positive space I live in today.

Since I've made these changes, I've made new friends and started new business opportunities. I have embarked on a relationship and I am living with the man of my dreams after being single for over ten years. My heart is overflowing with joy and I want to spread this message so that more people can feel this way.

MARISABELLE BONNICI

PHARMACIST, HOLISTIC NUTRITION AND INTUITIVE EATING COACH AND BINGE EATING RECOVERY COACH

roadtobelle.com

Marisabelle is a pharmacist from Malta. Between 2008 to 2010, she lived in the Netherlands reading for a masters in Toxicology and Drug Design. She returned to Malta and bought her first business at the age of 27 – a village pharmacy which she owned for five years. She battled a binge eating disorder for most of her adult life. In 2017, she started her journey to recovery from her eating disorder. Realising that her life in the pharmacy was aggravating her eating disorder, she decided to sell the business. She lost a total of 50kg, started working out and learned to listen to her body's needs.

In the meantime, she became certified as a holistic health and nutrition coach and intuitive eating coach and started a course in eating disorders. She has also recently learned she is suffering from celiac disease and is now in the process of learning how to tackle this auto-immune disorder.

She organises workshops and coaches people in their journeys to restoring their relationship with themselves and the food they eat.

DANDELION JAM OF JOY

❀

2 Tbsps of Acknowledgement

2 Cups of Fresh Dandelion Petals

4 Cups of Boiling Love

2 Cups of Gratitude Sweetness

2 Cups of Surrender Juice

4 Cups of Allowing Playfulness

❀

- Martine Werkhoven -

TRUSTING YOUR INNER LIGHT

Living with joy. What emotions come up for you when reading this sentence? Does it mean listening to the sound of your soul? Opening your heart enough so you can love more? Maybe it means living your higher purpose, leading to the finer energies of your life? Maybe it means honouring the light of your soul and living your life with delight, play and laughter? Or does it mean to stop believing in yourself and to stop trusting the universe? We all know there are many temptations to stop believing and trusting the universe and yourself, yet there are many reasons to continue.

It all started for me in the early 90's when I was 23. Major transformations happened in my life. I had decided to live in China and I was ready to take a risk and let go of my life in Europe. It was rare in those days to see a Western European woman make such a leap. My husband was Chinese and I had come all the way from Europe to live in China. I was fearless and completely open to experiencing different perspectives of life. Even my family and friends had not expected me to make such a big decision. But for me, that was my path of joy. I wanted more out of life and it would allow me to make my life more playful and colourful. It all felt natural to me and seemed to be what I had to do to feel joyful.

Soon after my arrival, I studied the Chinese language which was a bliss in itself to learn. The Chinese characters are like small drawings, each containing a lot of meaning. I also travelled to all corners of China. I was able to see every kind of landscape. Beautiful nature. I was living with contentment and accepted the flow of my life. There was absolutely no resistance within me to then, eight years later, be beautifully blessed with the birth of my two children. Their lovely European-Asian appearance, their smiles, their sweet gestures, their love and their unique way of connecting with me. All of that was my joy and grace. I was happy.

As the years passed by, I started to notice that I was living my life unconsciously. I had little awareness of the non-transparency in my marriage and I was missing a deeper meaning to life. Slowly but surely, I was losing the connection with myself and my inner light was diminishing. I couldn't manage to find peace with the differences in values between my husband and myself. We also had very different definitions of the meaning of love and living your light. I realised that as long as I continued to live my life unconsciously and pursue the role he had given me, our marriage would not collapse. However, I could not continue. I wanted to grow and have a voice of my own. I wanted to be heard and be loved. That was not the case. I was also walking around with a damaged heart. I had given my trust to the wrong friends which was followed by some very lonely years.

Despite this, I continued to believe in myself and to trust in the universe. I had genuine reasons to feel grief and to feel like a victim but I would not give in. I would continue to seek the light in the midst of the darkness. I was afraid and I was anxious but I would continue to trust in the power of love. I believe that joy can exist in every moment if you are willing to stay open and receive the good the universe has to offer. Joy keeps your inner world soft and light. It keeps you uplifted and playful.

Right after my studies in the Law of Attraction, I found the Awakening of Your Light Body program with Orin & Daben. The Awakening of Your Light Body was like a lighthouse for me, standing on the top of a sheer cliff. For a long time, I had lost direction of my ship and had forgotten the feeling of abundance and joy. I was used to living without love from a man and did not know how to break free from my marriage. After all, for about 10 years we slept in different bedrooms in the same house. Following the program with Orin & Daben, I met my new partner who - within two years - became my new husband. Due to feeling emotionally tired from Chinese culture, I had promised myself that I would not choose another Chinese person to be my husband but I couldn't help it. I felt loved and safe enough to slowly come back to my light. He allowed me to communicate openly and always encouraged me to be self-confident, to be true to myself and to say 'yes' when I meant 'yes' and to say 'no' when I meant 'no'.

There was more though to learn about myself, something that was rooted deeply within me subconsciously and I was not aware of. Continuing to seek within, I found that I had lived my entire life with codependency. It was the exact root of why I had attracted what I had attracted in my life. The sadness and shame I carried around, the quality of my first marriage, the wrong friends I had attracted in my past, the quality of my relationship with money and my relationship with food. Even my relationship with my children was affected by the codependency. It was hard to accept but extremely healing at the same time, because I had reached a level of awareness that I previously did not have and that made it so much easier to heal.

'Living life with joy' provided different meanings for me along my journey. It started with my new life chapter in China, followed by the sweetness of my two children to then becoming blessed with learning how to honour the light of my soul. For me, joy means being deeply connected to my loved ones and feeling loved. It means shining my light and growing, helping others to grow and shine their light too. It is living my life with a higher purpose and truly living the reason of why I came to this earth.

MARTINE WERKHOVEN

CERTIFIED LAW OF ATTRACTION & INTEGRATIVE HEALTH COACH

martinewerkhoven.com

With love for the laws of the universe and holistic wellbeing, Martine offers a unique blend of services that integrate the spiritual laws of life with digestive health and clean eating. She helps heart-centred women rewrite their pain stories and rebalance their gut health by looking into the power of the mind, emotions and conscious food intake.

Her personal story of overcoming emotional exhaustion, toxic marriage life and compromised gut health is the foundation of her business. She cultivated love for the Law of Allowing and uses this exact method to teach her clients which is in perfect alignment with the Law of Attraction and manifestation.

Martine has the gift of seeing the individual as a whole. She looks into self-love and forgiving of the self. She looks into diet habits, food and emotions and she provides you with actionable tools to nurture your everyday gut health. She's a strong believer in healing your body with gut-nourishing foods and feeding your soul and mind with the love and attention that it needs.

COLOURFUL LOVE PUDDING

1 Bunch of Happy Memories

1 Portion of Laughter

A Lot of Love

1 Jar of Hundreds & Thousands

2 Children with a Dash of Cheekiness

- Melissa Desveaux -

OVER THE RAINBOW

Joy is all around us but not everyone feels or notices it.

I've been to countries where people live very simple lives without expensive houses, cars or gadgets yet they are enriched with authenticity. I've seen sick people still managing to laugh and cry tears of joy. So why is it that not everyone experiences joy? I believe it pours down to our attitude mixed with the way we behave and combined with the way we've lived our lives.

One of the most joyful days of my life was my wedding day. It was like a jar of hundreds and thousands sprinkled on top of a cake. It was full of bright colours, butterflies and lots of laughter, a truly happy day for everyone.

Our first few years of marriage were great. My husband and I travelled a lot, bought out first house and spent a lot of time together which was all very exciting and new. As time went on, we saw the best and worst of each other. Some days we would laugh and work as a team, other days we'd argue and not even talk to each other. This put a strain on our relationship. It wasn't until we decided to start a family that we found our marriage was truly being put to the test. I wanted a baby so much and I was too naive to think anything could go wrong during pregnancy. Falling pregnant for the first time is a moment I will never forget. We were both ecstatic. I didn't think I could ever feel more excited than I did.

However, I miscarried after eight weeks and this marked the start of a not-so-joyful period in my life. After having two miscarriages and a stillborn baby, I wasn't the same person as I once was and our marriage began to change. Even though my husband was with me every step of the way, I felt alone. I felt like he didn't feel the hurt the way I did. If he did, it didn't seem like it.

Luckily, my sadness gave me profound determination and strength I didn't know I had in me. I started writing so I could keep a memory of my babies. Not only did this help me grieve, it became a passion of mine and something I continued to do throughout the birth of my son. Life became sweet again after my son was born. As I held him and looked into his eyes for the first time, a rush of pure happiness and love ran through my body. I cried tears of joy for the first time in a long time.

All the emotional and physical pain seemed non-existent in that moment. However, as I learned to adapt to a new chapter in my life, raise a new baby and care for my whole family, I started to feel lonely again. I began writing a blog about my pregnancies to pull myself out of my sadness. I documented my next miscarriage. From then on, I knew I had to do something to help other people like me. As I started meeting people from around the world, it was obvious that women in particular wanted someone to talk to about their pregnancy losses. I started comforting people I didn't know through their own loss and this brought joy into my life. I felt I was doing something meaningful for other people in a small way.

One year on from my last miscarriage, my second bundle of joy was born. I felt the same love and happiness as I did with my eldest son but again, it was not how I imagined it would be. I was disappointed that I didn't get to experience a natural birth again. I wanted to hold my baby after he was born. Yet I realised how blessed I was to have two children in my life whose happiness and wellbeing bring me joy on a daily basis.

After years of documenting my experiences on pregnancy and

pregnancy loss, I decided to write a memoir. I was proud of my achievement and felt a great sense of fulfilment in helping other women like me. I gave away my wedding dress so it could be turned into beautiful Angel Gowns for babies that left the world too early. Within a few weeks, I was asked to speak at the Angel Gowns Australia Charity function. Speaking in front of an audience was daunting and as I spoke my first words, I could feel my heart racing and nerves rising. The audience had all experienced pregnancy loss or were involved in the organization in some way. I could see in their eyes that they understood what I was feeling. Speaking openly about my experiences opened a new world of opportunities for me and added another ingredient to my life.

A few months later, I asked my already established social media audience if they would be interested in writing about their own pregnancy stories and many people replied. Their stories turned into a collection of memoirs that I self-published into a book. After trying my hand at different types of businesses, following different paths and often feeling confused and held back, I felt a burning desire to create another book. I finally felt my purpose and I reproduced a second version of the collection so I could help even more people.

My passion now is to help people self-publish their own books so they too can tell their stories. I know the joy that manifests when people are given a voice and a space to express their story after years of it living inside of them. My life-changing experience, my family, the people I have met and my books have all given me an understanding that happiness is always within reach, no matter the circumstances.

The ingredients to living a joyful and happy life are to cherish every day and everybody you love. Be yourself and do things that fulfil you. You don't need lots of material things to feel joy. Love, laugh and be kind.

MELISSA DESVEAUX

AUTHOR AND AUTHOR CONSULTANT

melissadesveauxconsulting.com

Melissa Desveaux is an author consultant, wife and mother of two boys. After experiencing the loss of four babies through miscarriage and stillbirth, she took the steps to grow a business, inspiring authors to write and self-publish their own personal stories.

As well as featuring in a number of publications, Melissa has written her own memoir and has compiled two books of stories written by women who have experienced pregnancy struggles. Her mission is to continue to reach out to women around the world so they don't feel alone in their grief after loss.
She has won an Australia Day Award for her dedication and commitment to helping families deal with pregnancy and infant loss and is a Support Ambassador at Pink Elephant Support Network.

Her children are her driving force. She aims to create a lifestyle that allows for more time to see the world and provides opportunities to learn from new experiences and make many joyful memories with her family.

THE ELIXIR OF LIFE

A Cup of Strong Spirit

A Measure of Courage

A Scoop of Curiosity and Wonder

A Hint of Rebellion

A Sprinkling of Heart Opening Cacao

A Whole Heap of Play

- Runa Begum -

BAKING UP DESTINY'S CAKE

As a little girl, joy for me was tagging along with my brother and his friends playing out in the backstreets of our neighbourhood. I fondly recall kicking around playing street games, sneaking in rules and tactics of my own, being raced down the street in abandoned shopping trolleys, one time hitting a pothole and unsuspectingly being catapulted out across the concrete. Running wild and bruised trying to keep up with the boys, the scars on my knees now boast the memories of those joyful years of my 80's childhood.

Somewhere in the cooking process, this little girl's joy began to fade with the prospect of life as a girl in a boy's world. A second generation Muslim Bangladeshi female raised in Wales, not only an ethnic minority to the majority world but at the lower end of the socio-economic stratum to the rest of her South-Indian counterparts. To top it off, a 'girl' to a family in the grip of its culture with fate seemingly predetermined by a patriarchal ideology that permeated through the layers of generational heritage. Left with a confused state of being and a puzzled sense of belonging, she questioned; 'Who was she? What was her value?' Slowly she infused in the growing process, becoming steeped in a picture frame of what it meant to be a girl.

The far-flung world for boys was a distant reach, as was her gaze into the lives of the masses, and beneath it all lay a hint of rebellion searching for an outlet. Looking in with curiosity, envy and even bedazzled eyes, she did feel a strange reverberation of a deep calling within; 'there's something more beyond this life, beyond what you think is written.' She wondered curiously; 'What was that echo? What was it connecting to in the vast expanse of space outside of her?' With the inability to make sense of it, she continued life as was predestined. A done deal, bound by the chains of fate, more so to the chains of her own making, she didn't even notice the light of joy dimming through those misplaced years into adulthood.

There is the other side though, the side that subconsciously tuned into the resonant vibration of that calling - which she now understands was the calling of her spirit refusing to settle. It artfully nudged and navigated her path out of the hole she was unwittingly helping to create. It opened up spaces of possibility, compelling her to step in bravely with an ever-growing conviction to pave a different path whilst mindfully balancing the tightrope of duty to custom and tradition.

Then came the chaos and upheaval with her very own big bang; she lost the patriarchal anchor in her life through the passing of her father. With unfulfilled obligations and responsibilities, potentially jeopardising the standing of her family, her world started to collapse around her. Unwrapping and unmoulding, old constructs came crashing down, de-fleshing and de-boning, preparing her to go inward to swim in the now gloopy melting pot of sludge that was the aftermath. Whilst trying to save herself from submerging, she came across a quote from Rumi that shone a crucial light - "When you lose all sense of self, the bonds of a thousand chains will vanish. Lose yourself completely, return to the root of the root, of your own soul."

Little did she realise in the alchemy of that deep painful dip she was to awaken to herself and recognise the call of her heart, beckoning to redefine old outdated ways. Led by an insight that her external world was a mirror reflection of her internal reality, now inviting her to become a purposeful participant in the grand design of life. As this truth unveiled, it began to ignite a spark within and so too reigniting joy, a joy that came from the pulsing of new life as she rose to walk the path of her own purpose.

Piecing life back together, she started creating a world of her own expression, this time using the ingredients of her choice. Think of it as a kind of sublime rose and cardamom cake baked up thoughtfully, lusciously layered with the most heavenly nutty butter-cream and indulgently crowned with glinting garnets of raspberries atop soft swirling peaks of coconut cream. A manifestation of her will, driven by the integrity of her spirit. An expansive world where curiosities deliver and lead to beautiful openings like fractals unfurling into portals, unending interweaving patterns akin to the infinite cascade of creation. A multi-dimensional recipe of life that is ever emergent, wondrous and vibrant, bringing joy alive. With this expanded creative state, openings revealed possibilities and previously hidden potential, bringing with them synchronicities that navigated the way forward - now recognising that this was her story and she gets to write it.

What I came to learn in this condensed version of an ever-simmering story is that joy is an emotion that is evoked from within. When ignited, it immerses me in a glowing warmth that radiates from inside, leading my heart and spirit into a state of happiness. It's that good feeling in my soul that connects me to experience the beauty of life along with its gifts of adversity.

It's not always easy though and I can lose faith. At times like this I remind myself that I have agency over my life and the ability to steer myself into a different state, cultivating the power to dream and to dream myself into being. I guess it's also important to feel the opposite of joy to truly know joy. The more I tune into joy, the easier I can shift into joy when I'm not feeling so joyful.

Somewhere inside, that little girl still resides. She continues to receive big squeezes of self-love and reminders that there are no coincidences, that we walk this path together, that fate keeps us in our comfort zone while destiny is created by taking risks. With enchanting sprinkles of heart-opening cacao, heaps of play and staying connected to beloved friends and family, she and I are cooking up our own Destiny's Cake with the finest elixir of life that is…Joy!

RUNA BEGUM

LEADERSHIP CONSULTANT, WAYFINDER AND LIFE FLOW COACH

runabegum.com

You can think of Runa as a 'master key' that unlocks human potential. Her effect on her clients is to awaken and liberate them – to help them to remember who they are, what they are here to do and why they're capable of doing it with total joy, passion and flow, and in so doing elevating the collective human experience.

Runa is a sought-after therapist, healer and coach. She straddles multiple worlds, bridging together expertise from the disparate fields of corporate leadership, contemporary therapy practices and ancient healing wisdom. She uses her unique combination of skills to break down limiting thought patterns and takes people below the surface to uncover what holds them back, replacing thinking with transformative being.

Runa's practices are grounded in her own personal growth as she continues to discover and reach through boundaries, bringing with her deeper wisdom, more clarity and joy into her own world.

NOURISHING JOY

✳

10 Portions of Fresh Whole Foods

Sweetened with Laughter and Singing

Sprinkled with Moving:
Dancing, Walking, Spinning, Jumping

Garnished with Gratitude and Quiet Time

(to feel and hear yourself breathe)

✳

- Susan Campbell-Fournel -

ON THE GARDEN PATH

I have experienced many moments of happiness in my life, but the moments I connect with true joy are profound and rest in my soul. Joy is an inner force, nurtured by moments of connection with our source energy of the universe. I experienced happiness when my new refrigerator and stove arrived, but joy is what I experienced when I held my first child in my arms.

Thirty years ago, the life I had known for 28 years was over. Divorce was never a part of my life plan. My generation married and lived happily ever after. Up until that point, I had followed the traditional 'life script' of graduating from university, getting married, supporting my husband and his career and balancing children and my career. I worked hard during those years convincing myself and others that this was happiness. There were times of happiness and joy but this script as a whole wasn't it.

During my transition from married life to single life I sought out therapy, knowing I needed a neutral guiding force to help me reach the next stage. Sadness, depression, resentment and anger crept into my life. Even though I had a Masters in Psychology and had been teaching at a small college in Montreal, I needed help. I did not want to be a victim of my circumstances or become a bitter old lady further down the road. I wanted to take this journey of transition and put things into perspective to rediscover myself. I needed to connect with the joy in my life: my faith, my daughters, my family and my friends. I needed to lift my eyes to the beauty of my surroundings and connect to my joy within.

I frantically read everything I could on recovery, divorce, stress, nutrition, religion, meditation and the body-mind-soul connection. One of the books that served as a tipping point for me was The Joy of Stress by Dr. Hanson. Since humans were first on this planet, life has been full of tasks, relationships and commitments. These elements of being human can't be eliminated but they can be managed and transformed into joy. I was determined to figure out how to rediscover the joy I felt growing up on Joy Road in Plymouth, Michigan. I indeed had control over whether I was going to be joyful or joyless. My reaction to life as it unfolds before me is paramount to discovering joy and the power it has in my life.

I began by converting once stressful activities into joyful ones. I found meal planning and preparation had become a burden. They were tasks which made me feel vulnerable and put my creativity, knowledge, self-worth, ability and skills to the test. Perceiving them all as a duty, I asked myself, "how can I make this fun?" Cooking and meals are an expression of love. If I keep my focus on the bigger picture such as anticipating the reactions of those I love or making my grandson's favourite meal, the whole process becomes a joyful one. It wasn't an easy conversion, but it was doable and it was liberating.

My new-found single status gave me the freedom to study and I wanted to know more about food and how it affects us. I grew up on a small farm and the foods we consumed, for the most part, were the foods we raised. My happiest memories are of being with my grandmother in her garden or kitchen. I loved putting on my sun hat to pick currents or standing on the small stool at the end of the large kitchen table to help her cook. Baking, canning, freezing foods, chopping, measuring, rolling dough, stirring and laughing. Oh, the smell and taste of joy!

My studies in nutrition revealed that the foods we consume impact our energy and moods. This in turn, impacts our perception of what is unfolding in our daily lives. Only during my university years, when I would drink copious amounts of caffeine to study through the night, was there a slight awareness that consuming something could alter your behaviour. It was a revelation to discover my mood and outlook could be altered by what I ate and even how I prepared it. Certain foods can help us sleep or raise our spirits. Taking the time to connect with the process and ingredients allows us to connect with the "spirit" of the foods we are consuming.

Julia Childs' Joy of Cooking shows that it's not just about the recipes but the love of the process. The preparation, smells, colours, textures and sharing with others. I began asking my clients to provide me with a food journal including when and where they ate. We discovered that by eliminating or adding certain foods and creating an enjoyable eating environment, a new and positive outlook about food began to form. This joy is knowing that our whole eating experience is nourishing each cell of our body and mind, bringing us closer to our potential. These powerful changes that take place by consuming the foods that nurture body, mind and spirit are now confirmed by food research. Mother Nature knew this all along, the joy of whole, natural foods.

Joy is an inner force that we must be proactive in nurturing. It is an internal resource that we can call upon to connect to the outer world. To leave happiness to chance or luck will leave us feeling empty and unworthy. We must reconnect with the inherent joy that we had within us when we were born. Poor food choices can interfere with this process. I have nurtured my joy with positive food choices and the realization that we are all connected to something greater than ourselves. You may call it God, the vortex, a universal spirit or simply a higher power.

I make morning walks my ritual. Watching the world awaken before the busy day begins allows my mind to connect and focus. Then I nurture my body and mind with whole-food nutrition, natural and clean, allowing me to tune in to a greater source of energy. It is this joy connection which frees us up to become greater than we ever imagined.

SUSAN CAMPBELL - FOURNEL

NUTRITION CONSULTANT AND COACH

susancampbellfournel.com

Susan Campbell-Fournel helps you discover the critical link between what you eat and how you feel. She is a former school psychologist, counsellor and college professor, with a Master's in educational psychology from McGill University. Susan, a Certified Health Educator and Coach became interested in nutrition and its impact on performance and achievement while working with children, young athletes and adults.

Public speaker, workshop leader, Susan is passionate about helping others achieve their goals and realize their purpose in life through a balance of nutritional awareness and mental focus. Susan incorporates the Juice Plus products into the nutritional plans for her clients, which enables them to "bridge the gap" between what they eat and what they need to eat to achieve optimal health for a sustainable lifestyle.

TEAM - JOY

A big thank you to these incredible experts that were working on this book.

SOPHIA IOANNOU - COPYWRITER AND EDITOR

PRITPAL MATHARU - BOOK DESIGN

SOPHIA IOANNOU

COPYWRITER AND EDITOR

Gutfeelingszine.com

Sophia Ioannou is a writer and editor from London with a lifelong love for words and stories. She began writing and travelling after finishing her undergraduate degree in 2012 and embarked on a career as a copywriter and editor while publishing zines on the side.

In 2013, she started up Gut Feelings where she is still the co-editor, collecting and publishing personal essays about life, love, people, travel and landscapes as well as conducting a series of interviews entitled The Brain Map, revealing the inner working of the brains of artists, musicians and writers.

Sophia has a passion for working with others to tell their stories and creates an inspiring, encouraging and safe space for authors to do so. After graduating with a Masters in Literature, Landscape and Environment, she is focusing her attention on narratives of place. She is currently creating a platform for female travel narratives by working with women to overthrow the male-orientated genre and create new stories that young girls can be inspired by.

PRITPAL MATHARU

GRAPHIC DESIGNER

letscre8.tv

Pritpal is a Brand Creation Strategist that helps businesses turn their visions into a cohesive and inspirational brand identity.

He tends to work closely with his clients to achieve high end designs that are bespoke, innovative and unique. Pritpal always strives to research current trends, using humour, creativity and endless imagination.

He has been instrumental in all creative aspects for the book. His mission was to produce highly impactful and stunning graphics. Spanning from designing the front cover to interior spreads and social media visuals.

Inspired by every story told, he created a variety of beautiful imagery that showcased every woman's recipe for Joy. Hence the flower theme throughout the book was introduced.

"Overall I'm very pleased with the end result, giving every story character, energy and purpose."

CHARITY

Through this book we are supporting a charity that will make
a difference to many other lives. We would be grateful for any donations.

CONNECTED SISTERS

CONNECTED SISTERS

my story

your story   our stories

CONNECTED SISTERS

justgiving.com/crowdfunding/connected-sisters

*Connected Sisters is a charitable organisation,
started by real life sisters Jodie and Paris Welton.*

*Their aim is to spread truth about the female experience in
the modern era. The duo gather real life stories from women all
over the world and present them daily on the Connected Sisters
platforms to help, empower and inspire other women.*

*One by one, each story challenges stereotypical representations of
women's lives prevalent across mass and social media, as well as
giving women a voice when they need to be heard.*

*The organisation regularly fund raises to help women in the
community. Paris and Jodie have been personally funding
Connected Sisters and welcome financial help. To support their
important work please donate using the link above.*

RISE

In Pursuit of Empowerment

- -

PART 1 OF THE GREATNESS STORIES

- -

We hope you loved the stories of Joy.
Why not grab the first book in this series?
Enjoy a further 25 stories of empowerment
and learn how these women have turned
their life around.
And if you would like to be featured,
get in touch for the next series.

REACH
FOR GREATNESS

★ www.learnmoreabout.info/rise ★

Made in the USA
Monee, IL
12 February 2020